Sussing Life

PERSONALITIES
SKILLS
HAPPINESS

Hamish Somerville

Sussing Life

Sussing Life describes in three steps how I have tried to follow the Oracle of Delphi's instruction to "Know Myself".

Personalities

Contemplating personality types helped me to understand myself and other people, develop my interpersonal skills and understand my inner nature. The word personality comes from Latin *persona* meaning a mask. Human beings are all made of the same stuff, but manifest with different masks, strengths, weaknesses, and habitual tendencies.

Skills

Contemplating personality types helped me recognise my strengths to build on and weaknesses and habits I needed to manage. Different personality types showed me clearly, how to improve a wide range of interpersonal skills.

Happiness

When I looked carefully within, I saw that behind my mask I am not my 'personality'. My thoughts, emotions, habitual reactions, and activities are what I do, not what I am. I see now that what I am is awareness or consciousness and I am encouraged to find that this view of life is supported by some leading scientists and non-scientific thinkers. Sussing Life has given me a happier understanding of myself, other people, and the world. May it do the same for you.

Hamish Somerville, Basel, November 2021

First published 2021
by Hamish Somerville / Sussing Life,
Glaserbergstrasse 21,
4056 Basel, Switzerland.
hamishsomerville@icloud.com

Printed in Great Britain

Cover design by Jim Kämmerling

ISBN 978-1-914195-77-8

For future generations and
especially for my grandchildren: Alba, Matilda, Emilia,
Aviana, Elliott and Louie.

Thanks to everyone who helped with this book.
Alison, Anitra, Anne, Babette, Christie, Doris, Gottfried,
Jim, Joyce, Misha, Trevor H, Trevor L, and many others
Special thanks to son Jamie for ongoing encouragement
and to Jay and Ruth at UK Book Publishing

May we all find lasting happiness

Contents

Overview

I was born in 1943 into a kind, loving, and generous family. As the third of five children, I was challenged to find ways to get attention from family and friends. I found several techniques that worked well for me. My main technique was to be a people-pleaser; smiling, friendly and helpful. Looking back, this technique and others helped me get the attention I craved and became part of my personality.

My lifetime obsession was and is to suss life, by which I mean understand myself, other people and the rules of the game of life. As a child, I was dissatisfied with materialism as a world view and convinced that before I reached twenty, I would find a new approach to life. At school, I had many kind, well-educated teachers. I read and learned a lot of history, philosophy, religion and science. However, in adolescence, with conflicting inputs from schools, religions, and media, I became increasingly confused.

Reflecting on people and personalities has helped me realise that the behaviours I developed as a child were habits that had, like all habits, upsides and downsides. As a simple example, the people-pleasing behaviour that helped me get attention created many problems including one of the biggest challenges of my life. I chose a career to please two important people in my life: one wanted me to study medicine and the other agriculture. As a compromise, to please both, I opted for veterinary medicine, which was fine, but got me into huge challenges dealing with what I see as the ignorance and

1

awfulness of humankind's treatment of animals. If this is new to you or you are not convinced, I recommend that you read *A Plea for the Animals* by French Scientist and Buddhist Monk, Matthieu Ricard.

After a few years of veterinary practice, I joined the pharmaceutical industry to work on developing medicines for animals. I enjoyed most of the work. However, when I was promoted to head of international veterinary product development, I found myself signing orders to test the safety of new chemical substances and candidate veterinary products in laboratory animals. As a child I had often asked myself how I would have reacted if, as a common soldier in the Second World War, I had been commanded to commit some of the atrocities of the holocaust. I strongly suspected I would have found ways to justify obeying orders. I had misgivings about animal testing, but I found reasons to go ahead and sign the orders. Now, in old age, I hope and believe I would be less likely to sign. To misquote Robert Burns, my sussing of life has included much reflection on "human inhumanity to men, women and animals".

The post-war culture I grew up in called itself Christian. This culture had supported both sides in two world wars, was addicted to economic growth and expansion, and was in essence materialist. The aim was always more. More food, more drink, more material goods, more cars, more planes, more packaging. More production and packaging meant more waste to be discarded in the environment. Little thought was devoted to the world we were creating for our grandchildren. I gradually became convinced that materialist thinking was taking humanity down the road to nowhere. What I learned at school didn't help me answer the big questions I had about life and about our materialist world view. I had to suss that for myself. Fortunately, I have lived most of my life in a time without wars in Europe and I had many opportunities to spend time contemplating and sussing life at home and on isolated meditation retreats. I still have a lot of sussing to do, but I have made progress and done my best to summarise the progress I have made in the three parts of this book.

Part 1: Personalities
Observing people and reflecting on a simple model of four personality types as the cardinal points on a human compass, gave me insights into myself and other people and how, although we are all made of the same stuff, we manifest in an infinite variety of different ways. We acquire behavioural patterns to deal with our life experience. These habits become our personality. Circumstances continually change. Habits remain habits. When circumstances change, our habits often no longer work for us and may work against us.

Part 2: Skills
Understanding personality types helped me recognise my strengths and weaknesses in everyday life and communication. This helped me to understand myself and other people and improve my interpersonal skills and my communication with other people. This understanding enabled me as a coach, to help others identify their strengths and weaknesses and improve their skills.

Part 3: Happiness

The word personality comes from the Latin word *persona*, for a mask. Our personalities are our masks, made largely of habitual behaviour patterns. When we see that our personality is a mask, we can look behind the mask and find, often to our surprise, that we are not our 'personalities'. We are not our habitual reactions or behaviour patterns. We are not our thoughts and emotions. Behind my mask is the real me, made of pure consciousness or awareness, free of habits and able to act appropriately rather than react habitually. That sounds simple, but it can take a lot of sussing to see it and even longer to begin to integrate it into life. When we see that we are not our masks, we face a challenging and essential question: "now we know what we are not, what are we?" For me, this is the most important, interesting and exciting question. I don't have the complete answer, but I have made progress.

My current aim is to adjust my mental computer settings so that consciousness becomes my default point of view.

Part One: Personalities

1 Personality Types

It started with a discussion over a business lunch in Basel, Switzerland. Dan Schwalbe and his colleagues had developed outstanding training courses for American employees of the multinational Swiss company that employed me for 25 years. We were discussing how to present the courses to employees in Switzerland. Someone drew and explained a simple model of four personality types on the back of the lunch menu. The discussion was a tipping point in my life and stimulated me to think deeply about myself, my behaviours and how I could learn from other people. I became increasingly interested in observing people and studying and contemplating personality types.

As an immediate benefit, I improved a difficult relationship with my superior. My bosses up to that time had mostly been enthusiastic, energetic and open. Working with them was fun. When I was invited to work in company headquarters, my style was accepted and I was soon promoted to the executive of my section of the global business. The problem arose years later with a new manager who was cool, goal-oriented, and ambitious, and expected everyone around him to be the same. He was not impressed by energy and enthusiasm. When I tried harder and increased the energy and enthusiasm that had worked well for me in the past, it made things worse. He didn't like my way of doing things, and he wasn't going to change. I had to change, but I wasn't sure how to go about it. I was worried about my future. The personality type model helped me out of deep trouble.

Seeing it from his point of view
The model told me that, if I wanted to keep my job, I had to see the world his way and from his perspective. Getting on with people who have power over us is much easier when we see life their way and think and behave like them. If we are not naturally like them, we are compelled to change our behaviour or risk being thrown out. On one management course I attended, this process was called the FIGO principle: "Fit in or Get Out".

Adapting is easier, if we are aware of personality types and how different people can be and how other people see us. After a lifetime of observing people, I am convinced that most of us tend to be happily ignorant of how other people see us. Robert Burns made this point after observing a smartly dressed lady in church. The lady was blithely unaware that a louse was enjoying life on the back of her elegantly coiffured head.

O, wad some Power the giftie gie us.
To see oursels as others see us!
—Robert Burns in To a Louse

We all want to believe we are right. Of course, sometimes our way is the right way, and their way is wrong. Often, their way is neither better nor worse, just different. Part of me wanted to think my new manager was a dangerous, ruthless dictator.

Deep down, I knew his style was just different and, in many ways, more effective than mine. I had to adapt to do things his way, find a new job or be pushed out. I started my campaign to adapt by demanding regular one-on-one meetings. Demanding was key to his communication style, and I did my best to match his poker-faced way of demanding. Objectives were crucial for him, so I made my goals clear at the start of each meeting with a clear agenda.

What I said and how I said it

I went straight to the point and demanded quick, clear answers to my questions, just as he always did with me. I leant towards him, looked him directly in the eye, and talked firmly and authoritatively, just like he did.

He had a habit of challenging the financial targets and project timelines for which I was responsible. If I said it would cost 300,000 francs, he would look me straight in the eye and retaliate with a significant reduction like 250,000. If a critical project step was due to finish in June, he would fix me with his gaze and reduce the timeline to April. I taught myself to look back, pause briefly to show I had thought about it, and if I saw no reason to change, I repeated my original predictions in a clear, strong voice.

I prepared simple visual aids to explain essential points to him. I laid the visuals out on the table between us to clarify my messages. The combination of telling and showing short, simple messages helped me be brief and direct and get my points across as he did. Our relationship improved.

The courage to change habits

This experience helped me to see that the reactive habitual behaviour of our personalities gets us into problems because it is reactive and habitual. We learn habits and acquire behaviour patterns that work for us. When we repeat these behaviours over time, they become part of our personality. Unfortunately, we go on repeating them when circumstances change, and the behaviours are no longer appropriate. I had to learn to adapt and act appropriately. I had to be less like my previous superiors and more like the new one.

Changing habitual reactions can be highly challenging and demands courage even when it's extremely urgent and necessary. Drug addiction is a good, albeit extreme, example. Addiction to nicotine, cocaine or alcohol is tough to overcome. As with all habits, the first step is to see the need to change and then find the determination and the courage to do something about it, including, in most cases, asking for help. The point is beautifully captured in the serenity prayer adopted by Alcoholics Anonymous.

God, grant me the serenity to accept the things I cannot change,
Courage to change the things I can,
And the wisdom to know the difference
—Reinhold Niebuhr

Personality in Ancient Greece

As we have seen, the word personality comes from the Latin *persona*, meaning a mask. Greek and Roman actors wore masks to amplify their voices and indicate their character and mood. With different masks, one actor played several parts.

Personality types are not new. The Greek philosopher Empedocles, born about 500 BC, attributed human characteristics to the influence of the four elements: earth, fire, air and water. Hippocrates, who lived a few years after Empedocles, is remembered in the Hippocratic oath taken by doctors and has been called the father of modern medicine. He recognised four personality traits he attributed to the predominant influence of four body fluids:

Four Types of Hippocrates
- Sanguine (blood): Cheerful and full of hope
- Phlegmatic (phlegm): Calm, not easily excited
- Choleric (yellow bile): Irritable, bad-tempered
- Melancholic (black bile): Gloomy or depressed

As we will see, types with markedly different characteristics, like these four, can be used as the cardinal points on a human compass to help us find our direction when dealing with different types of people.

Personality types in western psychology
The Swiss psychiatrist Carl Jung is regarded as the founder of modern personality typing. He observed many healthy and mentally ill people, reviewed the literature on psychological types and published his findings in 1921. His personality types are based on three pairs of personal characteristics:

- Extroversion and introversion
- Thinking and feeling
- Sensing and intuiting

Today, hundreds of models of personality types are available and are used to train leadership, management, teamwork, presentation, negotiation etc. Many are based on Jung's work.

The appearances and nature of mind

The Buddha taught 2,500 years ago that mind has two aspects. One aspect is mind's clear and unchanging inner nature. The other aspect is mind's constantly changing appearances and projections as thoughts, feelings, perceptions, sensations, and mental states.

Contemplating personalities and personality types has helped me to see that I am not my thoughts feelings, perceptions, sensations, and activities. These are what I experience, not what I am. I am the pure consciousness or awareness that experiences all of these.

Mind has been compared to film projectors, screens and to holograms in which awareness (mind's nature) is projected as images, thoughts, emotions sensations and experiences (mind's appearances) on a screen or in space as a hologram. Our culture teaches us that our dream appearances which seem quite real when we are dreaming are dreams that only exist in our mind and are not 'real'. Our culture is equally clear that the appearances of our waking life are real and exist as material parts of a material world. Sussing Life helped me to realise that all my daytime and dream experiences are appearances in awareness.

Our personalities are formed in three steps as follows.
1. Thoughts and feelings lead to actions
2. Successful actions are repeated to form habitual patterns
3. Habitual behaviour patterns form our personalities

These habitual responses are not inherently good or bad. The difficulty is that they are habitual and we continue to apply them when they are not appropriate. When we recognise that our personality is a mask, we can look behind the mask for the essential consciousness which preceded both our learned habitual reactions and the thoughts and feelings which formed them. If we discard our habitual reactions we can act appropriately to each situation and stop reacting habitually.

It came as a shock to me to find, as a mature adult, that my personality, which I had taken so seriously and regarded as 'me' and one of my most important possessions, is largely a collection of learned behaviour patterns. My behaviours are not what I am, but merely what I do.

What I am is the unchanging consciousness that lies behind the behaviours which appear as my mask. My persona or mask is the character I play when I project my thoughts, feelings and emotions in everyday life. We are all merely actors in the great play of life.

All the world's a stage,
And all the men and women merely players;
They have their exits and their entrances,
And one man in his time plays many parts

—William Shakespeare in As You Like It

Worldly concerns

Buddhist texts describe how our hopes and fears, the things we like and dislike, keep us occupied with materialistic thinking and prevent us from recognising our true nature. We are permanently busy chasing things we like, desire and hope for, or we are busy avoiding things we dislike and fear. The likes range from mild likes to obsessions or addictions, and the dislikes from mild dislike to hatred and phobias. Our hopes and fears can be classified as four pairs of opposites known as the 'eight worldly concerns'.

1. Hope for gain and fear of loss
2. Hope for pleasure and fear of pain
3. Hope for praise and fear of blame
4. Hope for fame and fear of insignificance

The words used to describe these hopes and fears may vary with the translations from the originals, but the meaning is similar. They include the worldly objects, substances, activities, relationships, and other things we humans hope for and seek and want to have, or fear and want to avoid having. When repeatedly experienced, these concerns become behaviour patterns and are integrated into our personalities. Put simply, if children are rewarded for being open and friendly, as adults they become open, friendly personalities. If they are rewarded for being quiet, careful, and withdrawn, they become quiet, careful, and withdrawn. We become attached to having what we like and not having what we dislike. Our likes become wants and then must-haves, and in extreme cases, we are addicted. The same happens with dislikes. People who dislike or fear things, for example, snakes, spiders, people of other races, sickness or poverty, can be just as attached as people who like and hope for gourmet food, wine, power, drugs, money or sex. As long as we are under the influence of our worldly concerns, we are attached. We aren't free.

Some habits, for example, washing, cleaning our teeth, and taking regular exercise, are inherently beneficial. Others become beneficial, as when an alcoholic acquires a habit of avoiding alcohol or a smoker takes to exercise and inhaling pure air. We learn behaviours because they help us survive. However, as already mentioned, problems arise when the behaviours become habits. When circumstances change, our habitual reactions may cause us problems. Worldly concerns are distractions that keep us from recognising our true self. From this point of view, we live in permanent distraction.

Distracted from distraction by distraction
—T.S. Eliot in Burnt Norton

We go to great lengths to defend our habits, masks and personalities as we desperately seek happiness and satisfaction outside ourselves when the answers are within.

The mass of men lead lives of quiet desperation
—Henry David Thoreau in Walden

Mind or matter?
Western psychology focuses on our thoughts and emotions, which are the manifestations, appearances and projections of

our minds. They are what the mind does and not what the mind is. Western materialist thinking, based on the belief that consciousness arises from the brain, is by far the dominant culture in today's world. The vast majority of human beings believe that mind arises from the matter of the brain. They think they 'are' the thoughts and emotions that originate from their brains. They see personality as something sacred, highly personal, connected to and located in the brain, and only describable with long words and technical jargon. As we will discuss later, scientists at the forefront of advanced physics who investigate sub-atomic particles, and religious contemplatives who spend years investigating the nature of their minds, come to the same conclusion about matter. They see that we, and our world, are made of and appear in consciousness. In other words, they see that matter, including our bodies and brains, arises from consciousness and not the reverse.

Contemplating personality types has colossal benefits. It helps us understand ourselves and other people, improves our interpersonal skills and brings us closer to seeing that our true inner nature is pure consciousness, peace, contentment, and happiness.

2 Profiles

Since the time of Aristotle and Socrates, many systems or models have emerged to type people. All models are approximations and inherently wrong, but some are highly useful. The Profiler on the following pages uses 15 simple questions and compares your answers, with typical responses of the four personality types to be described in the next chapter. Answering the questions before getting to know the types will help you avoid confusing how you are with how you would like to be. The inputs are yours and the outputs and conclusions are yours. Some sophisticated models use long words, computer programmes and statistical validation to produce long detailed reports; analysing, drawing conclusions and proposing actions based on your inputs or inputs of someone who knows you. These models can give the false impression that they are a precise analysis and that your personality is fixed and unchanging. Your personality is constantly changing. To profile yourself, answer the questions quickly and describe how you are, not how you would like to be. Note your answers to the fifteen questions then mark your profile on the table on page 23. If you have characteristics of more than one type, feel free to mark several types. If you have reason to make several profiles, for example, if you would like friends or colleagues to profile you, make copies of the table before you start so you can make several profiles.

PROFILE YOURSELF

First Impressions

1. How do you most like to dress?

    1. elegant and smart

    2. conservative and quiet

    3. comfortable and relaxed

    4. different and striking

2. How is your body language?

    1. few reserved gestures

    2. open friendly gestures

    3. many active and energetic gestures

    4. few emphatic, assertive gestures

3. How do you keep your personal space?

    1. organised and tidy with information to hand

    2. comfortable and cosy with photos of people

    3. signs of multiple energetic activities

    4. impressive, symbols of status

PROFILE YOURSELF

Motivation

4. What motivates you most?

1. friendliness, harmony and safety

2. fun, excitement and recognition

3. achieving results, gain and status

4. security, reliability and being right

5. What do you dislike most?

1. losing and being seen as a loser

2. being criticised for making mistakes

3. conflict and aggression

4. boredom and lack of activity

6. What motivates you to take on a task?

1. clear objectives

2. challenge

3. friendly atmosphere

4. clear procedures

PROFILE YOURSELF

Character

7. Which word describes you best?

    1. friendly

    2. determined

    3. reliable

    4. enthusiastic

8. How do you deal with risks?

    1. if it sounds like fun, go for it

    2. can be dangerous, analyse carefully

    3. be careful, or people may get hurt

    4. if the gain is bigger than the cost, go for it

9. How do you make decisions?

    1. slowly after weighing up the details

    2. quickly on gut feeling

    3. quickly on overview

    4. slowly on agreement and consensus

PROFILE YOURSELF

Communication

10. How do you communicate?
   1. relaxed, unhurried, open and friendly
   2. direct and straight to the point
   3. fast with energy and enthusiasm
   4. carefully with attention to detail

11. How do you complain?
   1. forcefully with few words
   2. logically with details
   3. gently and politely
   4. energetically and loudly

12. Which describes you best
   1. listens, interested in opinions
   2. talks, interested in facts
   3. listens, interested in facts
   4. talks, interested in opinions

PROFILE YOURSELF

Teamwork

13. How might you irritate people in a team?

    1. too many ideas

    2. soft and indecisive

    3. reserved and not participating

    4. selfish and bossy

14. Which focus would you bring to a team?

    1. results

    2. procedures

    3. harmony

    4. novelty

15. Which is your team strength?

    1. care for people

    2. ideas

    3. focus on results

    4. attention to detail

YOUR PROFILE

	Harmonizer	Enthusiast	Boss	Checker
First Impression				
1 Dress	3	4	1	2
2 Gestures	2	3	4	1
3 Surroundings	2	3	4	1
Motivation				
4 Positive	1	2	3	4
5 Negative	3	4	1	2
6 With Tasks	3	2	1	4
Character				
7 You in a Word	1	4	2	3
8 With Risks	3	1	4	2
9 Decisions	4	2	3	1
Communication				
10 Normal	1	3	2	4
11 Complain	3	4	1	2
12 Talk/Listen	1	4	2	3
Teamwork				
13 Weakness	2	1	4	3
14 Focus	3	4	1	2
15 Key Strength	1	2	3	4

Reflecting on your profile

Nobody fits perfectly to a type. We are all unique with unique behaviour patterns, and our habitual reactions are not inherently right or wrong. Some of us have strong characteristics of one type and others have characteristics of several types The big question is; how appropriate are our behaviours, in the situations that we deal with every day? Our past development may not have prepared us to deal with present circumstances. If we compare the pattern of our answers to our life experience, we will inevitably find occasions when our behaviours were not optimal or appropriate. So, the next question is, what can we do to improve our ability to act appropriately. Changing is up to us, but with the compass and our profile, we have a rationale for change. It is an illusion to think that we don't or can't change. Our personalities contain habit patterns, and habits are persistent, but they are not cast in stone. We can and do change.

Especially if you are no longer young, you may find you have acquired more than one mask. One good friend clearly describes several different masks for different parts of his life. One for his senior management job, one for his role as a father, and a third for playing tennis and so on. Another friend found she had different masks for playing as a professional musician, for hillwalking and teaching languages. I suspect many of us have different masks for different situations. The fact remains that even if we have different masks, when we don one mask, we react with the habits belonging to that mask.

Our habitual behaviour patterns are not the 'real me' and are not always appropriate.

In summary, we can group people with similar behaviour patterns as one personality type and present each type as an exaggerated stereotype. One aim of this book, and especially the next chapter, is to help you develop and internalise a people compass with four extreme types as the four corners. As we will see, our four types can be presented and roleplayed on video as exaggerated stereotypes – extreme examples.

One benefit of such a simple model is, you can carry it with you in your head to use in everyday life. Another benefit is you can check that the model matches your experience of human beings and makes 'sense' to you. If it doesn't, modify it accordingly. It's then your compass and a powerful tool to help you understand people, improve your interpersonal skills and find happiness..

3 The Compass

I would not for anything dispense with this compass on my psychological voyages of discovery
—Carl Jung

In the company I worked in for 25 years, employees were allocated personality types with the four-type model I was introduced to by Dan Schwalbe. We talked openly and joked about our types, our behaviours and our perceived strengths and weaknesses. Repeated exposure to the same model of personality types helped to create a customer-oriented company culture with high levels of job and customer satisfaction. Employees supported each other in recognising strengths and improving skills. The personality types presented here are like, but not the same as those of Hippocrates or Dan Schwalbe. In a similar way, they sort people, who appear in infinitely different guises, into groups that help us understand how people think and how best to deal and communicate with them. The compass is a simple, user-friendly tool to understand ourselves and other people.

Four cardinal points
The cardinal points on our compass are labelled feel, think, listen and talk. Of course, we all feel, talk, think and listen, but some of us feel more than think, some listen more than talk, and so on.

Four cardinal points on a personality compass

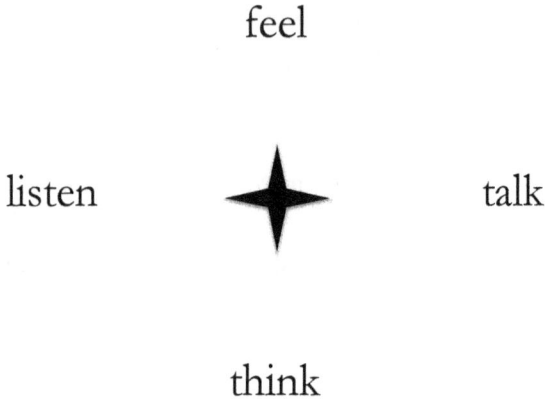

feel

listen   ✦   talk

think

To expand on these points. In the North, people who feel, tend to be open with feelings, people-oriented, intuiting, and warm. People in the South think more than feel and tend to be more task- than people-oriented. They are more interested in objects than ideas and give a cool impression. In the West the listeners are receptive and take time to gather information before making decisions or taking risks. People in the East talk more than they listen, are more assertive, more risk-friendly and make quick decisions.

Four personality types
The four types are positioned between the two cardinal points on the compass that have their main characteristics:

Four personality types between four points

Harmonizers
listen and feel

Enthusiasts
feel and talk

Checkers
think and listen

Bosses
talk and think

Conforming to type

Nobody conforms exactly to a type. Some conform better than others. Most of us have characteristics of several or all types. However, others may perceive us as having strong characteristics of one type. People change all the time for the strangest of reasons and it's misleading to describe personalities as if they were cast in stone. Working with the compass and with people from different cultures and backgrounds has helped me appreciate that other people do not think or feel like I do. Seeing this has helped me develop understanding, tolerance and empathy and realise that we can all benefit from understanding personality types.

What the four types like and seek

Harmonizers

harmony
comfort
consensus

Enthusiasts

excitement
novelty
recognition

accuracy
detail
reliability

status
gain
control

Checkers

Bosses

Key Motivations

These compasses show some of the key primary motivations of the four types in terms of what they like and seek and dislike and avoid. Enthusiasts´ and `Bosses´ are motivated to take risks and seek what they like whereas `Checkers´ and `Harmonizers´ are motivated to avoid risk and to avoid the things they dislike. However, we all have things we like and seek, and things we dislike and want to avoid. The goal of a `Boss´ to make a gain is in some ways similar to a `Checker's´ goal to avoid loss, but the motivation is different and the way to the goal is different. `Bosses´ aim to make gains, for example by taking calculated risks whereas `Checkers´ avoid losses by avoiding risks.

Motivation: What the four types dislike and avoid

Harmonizers	Enthusiasts
suffering	boredom
hassle	details
conflict	structure

failures	aimlessness
errors	delay
losses	losing

Checkers	Bosses

People of the same type can be very different. Some are extreme versions and some mild versions. Some of us have extreme characteristics of one type. Others have milder characteristics of several types. Some people think personality is something sacred and unchanging. However, the truth is that our personalities are largely habitual patterns. And, as most of us know well, changing habits can be very difficult. However, the fact is that our thoughts, emotions, and our personalities change constantly. Some personality tests go into great detail and, in my opinion, give the misleading impression that our personalities are fixed and unchanging. Our behaviours are constantly changing. and seeing this offers a huge opportunity for self-development.

Roleplaying the four types

As a manager and coach I found that roleplaying was the best way to help myself and other people understand and learn from the four types. To introduce the four types to new audiences I made simple, low-cost videos of myself playing the four types as businessmen. People from different backgrounds who have seen the videos agree that there are men and women of all races, ages, and nationalities who think and behave like the four types in the videos. Roleplaying to make the videos was great fun and helped me understand myself and other people, empathise and interact with people not like me. I have no training or experience in acting and the low-budget aspect and feel of the videos help to make the point that we can all learn to roleplay different personality types.

We all have different points of view, but as Hippocrates showed 2500 years ago, people can be grouped in ways that help us understand them and empathise, communicate, and deal with them. We can discover our own strengths and weaknesses and see how much we can learn from other people, especially those we find difficult, because they are not like us and have strengths we lack.

If you haven't already, you can develop your own model to match your experience of people. Your model will not be exactly the same as mine, but it will hopefully make sense and be of use in everyday life. Women and men of different ages and backgrounds do not see the world like the middle-aged businessmen in the videos, but there are people of all shapes and sizes with similar characteristics to the types in the videos. To get maximum benefit, watch the YouTube videos while reading the video texts below.

YouTube Videos

Go to: YouTube then search for hamish somerville then click on the name or the photo.

The video titled *'Sussing Life* explains in 10 minutes the rationale of this book and the four types. In the four videos: with the titles *'How to be a `Harmonizer'*, *'How to be a Motivator'*, *'How to be a Boss'* and *'How to be a Checker'*, the four types explain their characters in about four minutes each. Making and watching these videos, reading, and reflecting on the texts and roleplaying the four types, helped me more than anything else to understand personality types, understand myself and deal with people who are not like me. Hopefully the videos will do the same for you and you will see your strengths and weaknesses and how to get on with people who are not like you by adapting to be like them. At the same time, you will develop new interpersonal skills and empathy.

Video Text: How to be a `Harmonizer´ – Be like Harry

What kind of person am I? I'm a people person. I recognise that it's people who make a business and successful business depends on motivated people – people who enjoy their work. I believe that time spent creating a good atmosphere is important. Working relationships matter to me. I like harmony, and I like to take time. I like to get to know people. I dislike fighting and unpleasantness.

Motivation: I'm motivated by harmony, and I avoid hassle. I like to see people enjoying themselves and achieving. If people are happy and motivated then results follow.

Leadership: I believe the key to good leadership is to create a relaxed atmosphere, which motivates and stimulates creativity in the team. I believe in positive feedback. People respond to praise and encouragement. Picking on small errors and criticising discourages people. After all, making mistakes is part of the learning process. I don't really like using power, and I have difficulty sometimes to give people orders.

Teamwork: I really like participating in teams. I enjoy working with people. I'm very helpful, and I enjoy doing things with others. I can be a real diplomat in sorting out problems. I believe that people working together effectively in a team get results.

Decisions: Before making a decision, I believe it's important to obtain the views of the people who have the best understanding. I try to exploit the strengths of each member of the team, in order to reach sound decisions and to ensure everyone buys in.

Body Language: My gestures are like I am, warm, open, and friendly. I want to make a relaxed and friendly impression. If you watch me, you'll see that I really listen to what you're saying. I hope I give the impression that I'm friendly and approachable. My voice is also warm and friendly and soft. I want to make you feel comfortable.

Workplace: My office is a place for people. It's comfortable. Not over organised or clinical. There are photographs and things which show my interest in people.

Risks: I'm not one for taking unnecessary risks, unless everyone is in agreement. When we start taking risks, people get hurt. We can damage relationships, and that's exactly what we ought to avoid. Isn't it?

Wavelength: If you want to get on with me, be like I am. Take things easily and slowly. When I first meet someone, I like to spend a few minutes talking about trivial things, finding points of common interest, before we discuss business.

Persuasion: If you want to convince me about your product or idea, show me that it's safe and it's easy to use. People's opinions matter to me. So, if I know that other people are convinced, I'll give your product or idea a try.

Video Text: How to be an 'Enthusiast' – Be like Ernie

I'm an 'ideas' person. I've got lots of ideas, lots of energy. I like to get on with things. I like other people who like to get on with things. I don't like doing nothing.

Motivation: I like things that are new and exciting, interesting people who have ideas. I like lots going on around me, and I don't want to be bored. I might even enjoy a bit of a fight. But it's all-in fun. I start a lot of things, and I may not finish them all. I like challenges. I expect recognition for what I do. My motivation comes from the fun and excitement of dealing with new things. New ideas. I like adventure. I'm a bit of a daredevil. A few risks add spice to life. That's me.

Leadership: I enjoy working with people. I really like to get people going. And I know how to be enthusiastic and get others to be enthusiastic too. I'm a challenging person to have as a boss because I've got so many ideas. You may think I change my mind a lot. But that's because I'm always seeing new ways of doing things. I might even like to tease you, but I've a sensitive side, and I'm aware of hurting people.

Teamwork: In a team, I'm the ideas person. I'm very creative. I've got lots of ideas. Some of my ideas may turn out to be crazy, but so what! I've got lots of energy. I may talk too much and, perhaps I take the team off at a tangent. But we have fun! And it won't be boring when I'm in the team.

Decisions: I like to make decisions. I make a lot of them. I don't need a lot of facts, either. Just give me the basics, and I'll decide. If necessary, I can be flexible. I can change my mind too. You usually find a better way of doing things if you just keep looking.

Body Language: I'm active. I'm energetic, and it shows in my body language. Some people think I'm hyperactive and I jump around like a mosquito. I like to get things going. So I use a lot of gestures. Big gestures! Open gestures, showing my willingness to take on new ideas. But if I'm fed up, if I'm bored or hurt, you'll see that clearly in my body language too. My voice is energetic, and you can hear when I get worked up about things. If I'm excited, you hear it, and if I'm depressed, you'll hear that too.

Workplace: My workplace is somewhere to do things. I'm always busy, and you see that where I work. There are lots of signs of activity, signs of my many interests. Some people think it's chaotic. It's not really. There's just a lot going on.

Risk: Risk and challenge are what excite me most. If there's a mountain in front of me, I'm going to climb it! I really like adventure and things that involve risk. I'm a risk-taker. I can stand a lot of pressure, and I don't mind conflict. In fact, I hate to be without a certain amount of it, and if it isn't there, I'll often try to create it. I enjoy a good argument. Stimulates the mind.

Wavelength: Just be like I am. Be enthusiastic with lots of energy, lots of ideas and, for goodness' sake, don't be boring. But, be prepared to hear about what I'm working on right now. It's a great idea! I've got lots of great ideas and if you see that you'll get on with me!

Persuasion: If you want to sell me an idea or a product, tell me what's new and exciting about it. If you're excited about it, then I'm more likely to be excited too. If you ask me for ideas, I'll tell you how to sell your product and you'll find it easier to convince me with my ideas than with yours.

Video Text: How to be a `Boss' – Be like Bert

I'm an achiever. I want to win. I also want other people to know I'm an achiever. I like to be in charge of things. I'm goal-oriented. I set clear goals, and I stick to them. I rarely change my mind, and I hate changing decisions. If I have to use power and hurt other people to achieve my objectives, I'm prepared to do so.

Motivation: Gain, what's in it for me! That's what motivates me, and I'm not ashamed to admit it. I enjoy status, and that's also a driving force. I'm competitive. I want to get on and win, and I want to do it quickly. I hate it when people waste my time.

Leadership: I see myself as a natural leader. I like to take charge of things. I know how to set goals, and I know how to reach them. I'm not afraid to tell people, if they're not up to scratch. Is that clear? If you are not doing your job right, I'll let you know!

Teamwork: I have some doubts about teams. I don't believe they are always the best way forward. They can waste time and decision making is difficult with a lot of people involved. Teams work best when I or somebody like me is in charge. **Decisions:** I have no problem making decisions. Shows that I'm in charge. Tell me the costs. Tell me the benefits, and I can decide really quickly. I don't need a lot of facts. Give me the overview. That's enough.

Body language: My gestures are like me. They're strong, they're clear and they're to the point. You won't see much emotion in my body language unless I am really upset. My messages are direct. I look you straight in the eye and I tell you things as they are. My voice is like my gestures, strong, clear, consistent.

Workplace: My office is like me, it's organised, and it's business-like. You may see some signs of achievement or status symbols. I'm proud of my achievements and I want other people to be aware of them. I like status symbols. After all, I'm an important person.

Risks: I have no problem taking risks, but I make sure that they're calculated risks, where I clearly see the advantages and the disadvantages. If you don't take any risks, you never achieve anything.

Wavelength: To get on my wavelength, be like me. Act in a business-like manner. Be clear about what you want to say and get straight to the point. Give me the bottom line, what's it going to cost, what's it worth, how quickly can I expect results.

Persuasion: to convince me about a product or an idea, show me what's in it for me: Tell me how I can make a gain. Is there a financial profit in it? Will it give me recognition? Will it give me status? Can it be done quickly and efficiently?

Video Text: How to be a 'Checker' – Be like Charlie

I do things thoroughly which, of course, takes time. By working through the details, I avoid mistakes. I tend to be cautious, and I see all the potential problems. If I say I'll do something, I do it. If I say something will work, I know it will work.

Motivation: Security and the feeling that a job's been well done in a thorough fashion – that's what motivates me. I really want to get things right, and I want to avoid mistakes.

Leadership: I don't feel a great need to be a leader, but if I have to take the lead, to get the job done, then I'll do it. And as a leader, I'll tend to be careful. My actions and decisions will be well thought out, and based on hard facts.

Teamwork: When working in teams, I'm reliable. People can depend on me to do things right. I'm very good at checking details.

Decisions: My decisions are based on careful analysis. I know that takes time, but my decisions are well-considered and safe. Quick decisions often turn out to be unrealistic, and they lead to problems. I don't like that.

Body language: I don't make a lot of gestures. I don't see any need to get emotional. I normally adopt a neutral posture and a thoughtful look. That shows you that I am listening and trying to grasp the facts. I speak in a careful and measured way, slowly and quietly.

Workplace: My home, my office and wherever I work is always neat and tidy. As you know, I'm interested in details, so my workplace is full of highly organised information.

Risk: I believe that risks should be reduced to a minimum, and this can be done by using logic, by checking the facts, by carefully considering the options.

Wavelengths: to get on my wavelength, take your time, be prepared to discuss details. Show me facts that support your arguments. Whatever you do, don't rush me.

Persuasion: When it comes to products or ideas, I'm looking for security, so any kind of guarantees you can give will help. I prefer the tried and tested solutions. I know they work.

Can you do better?

These videos have helped me and other people and can help anyone who is interested in developing themselves to understand themselves, improve their skill sets and realise that they are not their personalities and that there is another me behind the mask of personality. Making the videos was great fun and gave me some great insights into how I think and how and why other people think like they do. You may decide to make your own videos of four types, either with my text or with your own types and texts. If you do, please consider allowing your videos to be uploaded. It would be great to have videos of people of different ages, genders and nationalities playing the types. Contact: hamishsomerville@icloud.com

All models are wrong. Some are useful
The compass is a model. Like all models, it's not reality. We need to remember that people and circumstances change and we may need to adjust our assessments of individuals.

The map is not the territory
—Alfred Korzybski

Intuition can and often does lead to better decisions than precise information. In Malcolm Gladwell's book, *Blink: The Power of Thinking,* in one example he describes how expert intuition of experts assessed the authenticity of a Greek statue much better than analysis of data. When shooting at targets, working with data, or trying to identify personality types, too much precision may completely miss the target. Accuracy in locating the target is more important than precision.

It is better to be roughly right than precisely wrong
—attributed to John Maynard Keynes and others

Stick to one model
One company I know used five personality models in courses on leadership, decision-making, presentation, writing and negotiation skills. All five evaluated similar characteristics with different words. Participants had to learn five vocabularies. Focusing on one model or compass for all skills offers colossal benefits. By all means, use your own model, but stick to one model. It will make life easier. In organisations, focus on one model helps to develop a common culture.

Putting People in Boxes

Personality tests like our compass put people in boxes. It is often said that it is dangerous to put people in boxes and, of course, we may put them in the wrong box. The fact is, however, we put people in boxes all the time. We make judgments about people within seconds of meeting them, and continue as our relationships unfold. However, we need to be aware that we are all constantly changing and may have different personality masks for different situations. Some people behave differently with men and women or with superiors and subordinates. This compass is based on logic and is more likely to be useful than uninformed guesses or assumptions. Personality types are fun, but the key benefits come from getting to know ourselves and other people and recognising that we all have strengths that are useful in certain circumstances, and we can build on these strengths. At the same time we all have potential weaknesses which manifest as habitual reactions. The aim of this book is to help people to help themselves by contemplating personality types and recognising the skills and strengths they need to improve and the habits and behaviours they need to change.

Strengths to work on and areas to improve

The table on the next page offers an opportunity to tick some boxes to recognise some of your strengths to work on and potential weaknesses to overcome. The list is by no means complete!

STRENGTHS		TO IMPROVE	
Harmonizer			
Listening		Assertiveness	
Diplomacy		Saying no	
Teamwork		Decision making	
Finding consensus		Unnecessary activities	
Giving support		Objective setting	
Enthusiast			
Vision		Too many ideas	
Creativity		Lack of structure	
Enthusiasm		Too much risk	
Energy		Starts not finished	
Risk-taking		Chaotic organisation	
Boss			
Assertiveness		Listen to others' views	
Set and get objectives		Inflexibility	
Persistence		Finding consensus	
Decisions		Overlooking details	
Overview		Dictatorial	
Checker			
Gathering information		Analysis paralysis	
Attention to detail		Slowness	
Reliability		Risks and decisions	
Logic		Delegation	
Planning and structure		Creativity	

4 Adapting

Human beings are all made of the same stuff, yet we manifest in vastly different ways and see things from different perspectives. I'm sure I had minor difficulties with people who were not like me as a child, but my `Boss´ boss was the first to cause me to change my behaviour in a big way. Personality types and my compass helped me deal with that situation and understand the differences in our points of view. I learned a lot about myself. When I started coaching, roleplaying different types helped me to understand the principles of adapting that we look at in this chapter.

With practice, we can learn to adapt our personality and communication, both verbal (what we say) and non-verbal (body language or how we say it) to be like our discussion partners. When we do this, our mindset adapts too, and we find it easier to understand their point of view, and they find it easier to understand us. Adapting does not mean we accept they are right. It means we adapt to get on their wavelength, pay close attention to them and are open to seeing things their way. Of course, adapting to others is not always appropriate. Sometimes the others are in the wrong, and it is clear we have to either stand up and tell them they are wrong or disconnect. In some communication processes, such as giving orders or commands or giving bad news, looking for agreement is counterproductive. Adapting is the way forward when we look for consensus as I had to do with my new boss. In such cases, a personality compass is an excellent tool to help with adapting and adapting is a good way to find agreement.

The boss with whom I had a problem was between a `Boss´ and a `Checker´. I was between an `Enthusiast´ and a `Harmonizer´. We were bang opposite each other on the compass. My first automatic reaction was mistaken and counter-productive. As many of us do, I reacted the wrong way by reinforcing my normal behaviour. This only drove us further apart. When I understood the problem, I responded by being more like him. When I did that, the relationship improved. To get on with other types, the basic rule is to be more like them and less like you. It sounds obvious, but experience and discussions with other people tell me it's a hard lesson for many of us to learn.

How to adapt to be like the four types
To be like a `Harmonizer´ slow down, reduce power, be open and prepare to talk about opinions and feelings. Relax and lean back, using open gestures and a warm, friendly voice. Listen more than talk. Dress for comfort and avoid elegant or striking styles or colours.

To be like an `Enthusiast´, wind up the energy and excitement and get ready to expand your gestures and talk with energy and excitement. Be prepared to move about more and if you want to dress like an `Enthusiast´ go for outfits that are new, striking and different.

To be like a `Boss´ turn up the power, turn down the emotion, focus on facts, lean forward, smarten up, speak with a strong, clear voice, look your discussion partners straight in the eye and reinforce what you say with a few emphatic gestures. To dress like a `Boss´ normally means to wear expensive, usually formal, branded clothes.

To be like a `Checker´, slow down and turn down the power, the sound and the emotion. Take your time. Think before you speak, speak slowly and quietly with few gestures and dress like they do, which usually means dressing conservatively.

Mirroring

If you have an important meeting or discussion ahead and you know the type of person you are due to meet, you can use the information we have just discussed to prepare to adapt. During a meeting, when you are face to face, you can use the technique body language experts call mirroring.

Mirroring works on the principle that our mind matches our posture, gestures and facial expression. For example, if we take up an assertive forward-leaning stance, preferably with a height advantage, so we look down on them, it's easier to be proactive and assertive, like a `Boss´. If we take up a receptive posture, leaning back with open gestures looking up, it's easier to be open and listen like a `Harmonizer´ or `Checker´. When we deliberately match our posture and our height to our discussion partners, our mind adapts too, and we are more likely to find the same wavelength, and agreement is more likely.

When I first heard about mirroring, I thought my discussion partners would think I was making fun of them. However, with practice and sincerity, it works amazingly well.

You may think the other person will notice and be upset if you mirror them, but if you do it subtly and with sincerity, it goes unnoticed, and communication improves. When they lean forward, you lean forward. When they lean back, you lean back. When they cross their arms, you cross your arms. When they put their hands on the table, you put your hands on the table. People who are in love with each other seem to mirror each other without thinking. People who are gifted in communicating with young children find ways to mirror them from their level, for example by getting down on their knees. Non-verbal communication is much more important than many people think. As a light-hearted introduction to body language, I can recommend Alan Pease's videos on YouTube and his book, *Body Language: How to Read Others' Thoughts by Their Gestures*.

Adapting your voice

Adapting also includes adapting the volume, intensity, pitch and pattern of how we speak. We can use the same principle as in mirroring and adapt our voice to be like our discussion partner. To make a game of it, I allocated signature tunes to my key discussion partners. For a typical `Checker´, the theme might be a slow-moving, quiet piano concerto with lots of detailed notes. For `Harmonizers´, it could be a ballad or a romantic waltz. A loud and forceful anthem or a military march sounds right for `Bosses´. For `Enthusiasts´ with lots of energy, the music might vary in pitch and volume, and sound like rapping or bebop jazz. To illustrate the process of adapting, I've selected examples from personal experience.

Adapting to a `Checker´

I once had a colleague who tried my patience to extremes. He was a strong `Checker´. I liked him well, but I found his endless need to check details difficult. My obvious impatience with his interest in detail upset him and made communication difficult. I decided the only way to get on his wavelength was to prepare in advance. Before meeting with him, I went carefully through the agenda for our meeting, organised my papers and practised deep breathing for a minute or two. I continued the deep breathing as I walked slowly to his office two floors below mine. As I went down the stairs, I said to myself "slow down, slow down, slow down"! Before I entered his office, I took three long, deep breaths. Our meetings improved.

Adapting to a `Boss´

I once used my understanding of the compass at an important meeting with two technical colleagues. We had an appointment with a senior government official about the approval of a new product. It was a complex technical issue, and delayed approval would have meant lost sales and lost profit for our company. My colleagues had prepared detailed technical arguments and printed out visual aids to back up our statements. We were ready for a detailed two-hour technical discussion. None of us had met the official before. We arrived early for the meeting, scheduled for 10.00 am, and were told to wait outside his office. We waited and waited and eventually were invited into his office at about 10.25 am. The official we were meeting was sitting in a high-backed throne-like chair, behind an expensive and immaculately tidy desk. The surface of the desk was bare, apart from a blotting pad and a fountain pen. He gestured for us to sit opposite his 'throne' on a low sofa. From where we sat, we had to crane our necks upwards to speak to him. On the wall was a single, large, framed photograph. It showed our discussion partner at the top of a high mountain, holding an ice axe in the air.

We had prepared for a detailed technical discussion and were subconsciously expecting to meet a `Checker´, but all the signs said we were talking to a strong `Boss´. I signalled for my colleagues to leave the talking to me. In two or three sentences, I summarised how much we appreciated his valuable time and what we wanted and then asked straight out what we should do to get what we wanted. He paused for a few seconds, asked a couple of questions and then told us, in two minutes, what we had to do. We asked two more questions to clarify minor points, said our thanks and farewells and left. Despite a late start, we were ahead of schedule, and we fully achieved our objective! Had we shown him all our information, I'm sure we wouldn't have been as successful.

Adapting to an `Enthusiast´

My best lesson in dealing with `Enthusiasts´ came from a Dutch saleswoman who lived on a canal boat. Greta was a fan of personality types, and one day, she took me to visit a customer she described as a strong `Enthusiast´. She started by introducing me to the customer and telling me how enthusiastic he was and how many brilliant ideas she had picked up from him. She then briefly described an important new product and quite blatantly asked him how he would sell it to her if they changed positions. As a typical `Enthusiast,´ he couldn't resist the temptation to show off how many ideas he had. When he finally stopped talking, Greta quickly summarised what he had said and asked if the points he had made would convince him to buy. He said yes and bought the product. Greta made the sale look easy by challenging the customer to sell it to himself. `Enthusiasts´ love ideas and challenges, and if you can harness their creativity, it can help you and them. The idea to pitch the new product to an `Enthusiast´ made sound marketing sense too. `Enthusiasts´ as a group are known as *early adopters* of new products because of their love of novelty and excitement.

Adapting to a `Harmonizer´

I once had a charming and very talented manager with strong `Harmonizer´ tendencies. He was very good at asking questions and a great listener. In our one-on-one meetings, he would ask a question, listen and nod sympathetically in a way that encouraged me to go on talking. It took me some time to learn he wasn't agreeing; he was just listening. Like most people, I like it when someone listens to what I have to say. It was almost hypnotic. At the end of our discussions, as I came out of his office, I felt good. Then, as I got back to my office, I realised I had failed to get what I wanted from him. Our friendly meeting had been highly ineffective! I had adapted to his style by going along with his way of doing things, but I had not achieved my goals. The kind of adapting that worked with my `Boss´ manager, did not work with this `Harmonizer´.

It took me some time to understand that the best way to deal with him was to ask for help. As a `Harmonizer´, he liked to help, and he liked harmony and was very interested in other people's opinions. He wanted their agreement. I learned to check and point out wherever possible that everyone else who mattered, and especially people in positions of power, agreed with what I told him. He was a highly educated scientist, and it came as a surprise to me that other people's opinions were more important to him than technical arguments. Getting his agreement took time, but I started to come out of his office with clear commitments to my goals. He taught me to keep my objectives in the front of my mind while listening to `Harmonizers´. I learned to listen and stick to my objectives. I also learned to avoid being distracted by his questions and reassuring gestures. People with `Harmonizer´ tendencies like to help. Many of us underestimate how many people in this world like to be of help. Most of us would, I suspect, be more successful if we learned, on appropriate occasions, to ask for help.

Adapting in teams

On a leadership course, many years ago, I learned a lesson I will never forget. Participants were put into groups of six with an observer and a video camera to roleplay an emergency plane landing in the Arctic tundra. The passengers are all uninjured, but the aircraft will not fly, and the passengers and crew will not be missed for at least 48 hours. They must decide between two alternatives. They can build a shelter, make a fire, survive on minimal rations and try to attract attention with fire and a mirror, or they can use a rough map and compass found in the wreckage to cross a stretch of tundra to reach civilisation. The distance would be an easy hike over average terrain on a fine day. I enjoyed the exercise with my group, but the last group taught me my big lesson. This group comprised four young and very enthusiastic English-speaking `Enthusiasts´ and one shy and reserved analytical Austrian `Checker´ named Georg. Georg could speak English, but wasn't fluent and was a typical `Checker´. The video was spellbinding. The `Enthusiasts´ all wanted to go over the tundra. Each one had better reasons and ideas than the others. Every time one of them stopped talking for half a second, Georg tried, in halting English, to get a word in. The video showed his increasing frustration, which ended in despair when the time was up, and the group had decided to go for it. After we watched the video, the observer asked Georg what he had been trying to say. Georg answered slowly and hesitantly and with a strong accent: "I just wanted to say I've been a mountain guide for 20 years, and in that kind of country, in those temperatures and with our clothing, we'd be dead before we got there." The experts agreed with Georg.

Teamwork

Georg and the `Enthusiasts´ gave me a lesson in the value of teams with mixed personalities. They also illustrated clearly the need for different styles to appreciate, listen to, adapt to and learn from each other. The exercise confirmed several essential points for me. Working with people like us is fun. The `Enthusiasts´ had great fun supporting each other and reinforcing each other's opinions. We all enjoy working with people who are like us and think like us. When we reinforce each other's opinions, we feel good. However, it's the people who aren't like us and we find difficult, from whom we learn the most. In teams, those who aren't like us, especially those on opposite corners of the compass, have the strengths we don't have and compensate for our weaknesses. Communication involves both talking and listening.

The message for personality types can be put simply: `Harmonizers´ and `Checkers´ on the western or left of the compass have difficulty being assertive. They need, at least at times, to move east on the compass and find the power to speak up when they have something of value to say. `Bosses´ and `Enthusiasts´ find it easy to be assertive and often need to learn when to shut up and listen. Enthusiasm is great, but sometimes we need to reflect and listen before acting.

Georg illustrated how `Checkers´ can have valuable information for groups but may not be assertive enough to get their ideas across to `Enthusiasts´ and `Bosses´. Being right when everyone else is wrong is of no value if you can't speak up and convince others. The `Enthusiasts´ and their inability to listen was a big part of the problem, but Georg's personality also failed him. His lack of English didn't help, but that wasn't the primary problem. If he had been in a group of `Checkers´ or `Harmonizers´, I'm sure he would have made his point. In such a formidable group of non-listening `Enthusiasts´, his communication style was not powerful enough to interrupt them. Maybe he could have dealt with one such person, but a group of four was too much.

4 Adapting

Too assertive or too receptive
I've coached many young managers selected for promotion to top jobs. Their employers saw their great potential and recognised specific weaknesses they needed to overcome to succeed in higher management. The shortcomings of these management candidates fell into two main groups.

One group consisted of people who were like the four `Enthusiasts´. They were `Enthusiasts´ or `Bosses´. Their main weakness was a tendency to be over-assertive. They sometimes failed to listen and gather essential information for their activities. They needed to learn that assertiveness is not always appropriate. Leaders need to learn when to be receptive and listen. The other group I coached were people like Georg. They were `Checkers´ or `Harmonizers´ who had valuable knowledge and good listening skills. These people often had a fantastic track record as technical experts, problem-solvers or team players. However, they lacked assertiveness and put too much emphasis on consensus or detail. They needed to learn, when necessary, to move east on the compass and be more self-assured and assertive.

Adapting Power and Emotion
I am sure many of the people I coached also needed to learn to move North or South on the compass and become more, or less friendly and open with feelings. However, my experience says that for career development, adapting power by being assertive without being aggressive or being receptive without being weak is more of an issue than adapting feeling.

.

55

The best teams mix types

Teams benefit from a mixture of types. Teams with members of very similar styles can be potentially dangerous, as the `Enthusiasts´ illustrated in the exercise with Georg. Similar types get on well with each other, but that's not always what teamwork is about and may not help to make the team effective. Successful teams disagree with each other because they have different personalities and different ways of seeing things. That's not a problem. Conflict can contribute to progress. As a famous soccer manager once said: "I expect my team to disagree like hell, but I also expect them to keep the disagreements within the team and not to hold grudges."

Is there a best type for the job?

It's tempting to think one personality type may be best suited to specific jobs. For example, we might think `Checkers´ make the best accountants, as they have to deal with detail, but accountants sometimes need the skills of all four types. A finance department made up entirely of stereotypical `Checkers´ could be a disaster. Some people think `Enthusiasts´ have an advantage in sales because they like challenges and can deal with being turned down. Stereotypical `Enthusiast´ salespeople often have problems with reporting and administration. Details and paperwork are important too.

Experienced managers who should know better, often make the mistake of surrounding themselves with people like them, people of the same or similar personality types. After major reorganisations or takeovers, new managers often replace people with years of valuable experience and know-how with people like themselves who behave as yes-women and yes-men. Of course, this makes it easier to avoid disagreements, but it's dangerous for exactly that reason.

Conclusions on adapting and teamworking

When we have to give orders or do not want or need to reach agreement, adapting is not necessary or of benefit. Adapting helps and may be essential when we need to reach an agreement.

Playing the four types in coaching roleplays is fun and teaches us that we can learn to be flexible and change our habitual behaviours. Learning to adapt is a big step towards seeing that personality is a mask made of habits. It also helps to develop empathy. We learn to see things from our discussion partners' points of view. More importantly, we encourage them to see things from our angle.

Learning to adapt and mirror takes practice. Most of us feel uncomfortable when we start, so it's worth practising with friends before trying it out with important contacts. We all find it easier to get on with people who think like us, but we learn most from people who are not like us, and who have the strengths we lack, even if we frequently disagree with them. That's why strong teams include different types with different strengths.

When you don't have all the skills yourself, it may not be realistic to learn the skills. An alternative is to build alliances with people with the skills you lack. A team approach or a partnership with other people with different skills is often a useful and powerful way to balance individual weaknesses.

4 Adapting

Introduction to Part Two

Personality manifests as learned behaviour patterns. `Bosses´ learn to be bossy and ambitious, `Enthusiasts´ to be enthusiastic and energetic, `Checkers´ to be accurate and reliable, and `Harmonizers´ learn to be open and helpful. You learned to be your personality and I learned to be mine. To be effective in all circumstances, we need to stop acting habitually and start acting appropriately to new situations. The aim of Part Two is to see how we can improve interpersonal skills by overcoming our learned habitual behaviour patterns and acting appropriately to situations rather than reacting habitually. The focus is on skills I wish I had learned earlier in my working life and on aspects of skills that illustrate the importance of personality types. It is not intended as a skills manual.

Part Two: Skills

5 Leadership

In a way, we are all leaders. We all have responsibility for leading ourselves and we can all benefit from leadership skills. Leadership is a vast topic, but there are two leadership situations that most of us know. Most of us take part in meetings, and most of us have experience of family life and an understanding of parental responsibilities.

How the four types lead meetings

`Bosses´ typically organise meetings and stick to a meeting plan or agenda. They keep the meeting and participants under control and on track, and make sure actions are agreed upon, noted, and implemented. They see themselves as strong leaders. However, strong `Bosses´ are often not good listeners and may fail to listen to participants. At the end of a meeting with a strong `Boss´ in charge, participants often feel they've not been heard, and important information hasn't been discussed. `Harmonizers see strong `Bosses´ as steamrollers who force their decisions on meetings without discussion.

`Enthusiasts´ typically have lots of ideas and energy and make meetings fun, entertaining, and lively. Their enthusiasm is infectious, and an `Enthusiast´ can inspire participants to go in new directions and get new projects off the ground. Participants are unlikely to be bored. However, with their creativity and wealth of ideas, `Enthusiasts´ are prone to making frequent changes. They are often unstructured and may fail to plan and prepare meetings correctly or forget details. In extreme cases, they may not think it useful or necessary to prepare or stick to a formal plan or meeting agenda. They may forget to take detailed notes or minutes or note down agreed actions and make sure these actions are implemented. `Checkers´ find `Enthusiasts'´ meetings chaotic, unstructured, unreliable, and too quick to make decisions, without considering all the facts.

Harmonizers´ are great diplomats and are good at achieving consensus, listening to everyone's opinions, and maintaining harmony. When running meetings, they make sure everyone is heard. They are, however, often overly concerned about people and their opinions and not sufficiently focused on the objectives of the meeting. They may spend too much time listening to opinions and seeking agreement. As a result, they may lose sight of the goal and fail to keep to and complete the meeting agenda. Meetings run by typical `Harmonizers´ can run seriously over time, and trivial issues may be discussed at length, with no time left for critical topics. `Bosses´ see meetings run by `Harmonizers´ as wishy-washy and lacking clear objectives.

Checkers´ run structured meetings, pay attention to details, and make sure they have all the facts before making decisions. They may get lost in factual detail, and find no time for people issues, achieving goals or moving quickly through the agenda. They can be great leaders, but because of their interest in detail and their need to check details, meetings chaired by `Checkers´ often take a very long time to reach conclusions. `Enthusiasts' find meetings run by ´Checkers` slow and boring.

Parenting and personality

A quick look at parenting also illustrates why as leaders there are times when we need the strengths of all personality types. When children are in danger or behaving stupidly or sometimes just to get them to accept it's time to get ready for bed, 'Boss' authority is necessary. When children are hurt, suffering, or in pain, they need the support of a 'Harmonizer'. In helping with schoolwork, a 'Checker' approach is often required. The enthusiasm of 'Enthusiasts' can get children going so they have fun, enjoy themselves and develop creativity.

The quintessential point is that all of us, whether we are parents, leaders, great or ordinary human beings, sometimes need the leadership characteristics of all four types.

A leadership diamond

Peter Koestenbaum's *Leadership: The Inner Side of Greatness, a Philosophy for Leaders*, shows a leadership diamond. His four qualities shown on the next page are very similar to the qualities of our four types shown in brackets. Vision is the quality shown by our 'Enthusiast', Ethics is shown by our 'Harmonizer', realism is a strength of our 'Checker', and courage the strength of our 'Boss'. In the middle of the diamond is communication. The book argues that great leaders require the characteristics of all four points of the diamond and the communication in the centre. If all four characteristics and communication are not present, the diamond collapses.

Vision
(Enthusiast)

Courage   Communication   Ethics
(Boss)   (Harmonizer)

Reality
(Checker)

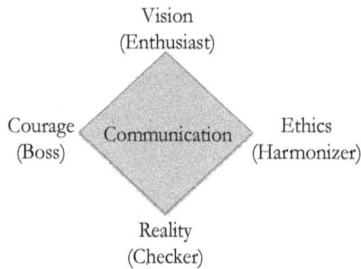

It's interesting to discuss how this theory fits great dictators like Hitler. He had vision and courage and was to some extent realistic, but he had serious problems with ethics and communication. He was an extreme `Boss´ type who didn't listen to advice he didn't want to hear. He lost contact with reality, ignored advice not to invade Russia, overstretched resources and suffered drastic defeat with appalling suffering.

Situational Leadership

Situational leadership describes levels of Direction, Autonomy and Support required at different levels of task performance and experience.

Direction: A beginner, at the bottom of the performance curve, needs mostly clear direction (`Boss´ approach) and little autonomy or support. This may seem surprising, but beginners need to get to grips with the basics when they start a new job or a new task. They need some advice and assistance, but support and coaching from above can be confusing to someone who is learning the basics of the job. Clear direction is essential.

Situational Leadership is about performance in individual tasks. People perform different tasks at different levels on the curve. For example, some Salespeople are great at selling and poor on paperwork. Some doctors are great on science, but poor on bedside manner and so on.

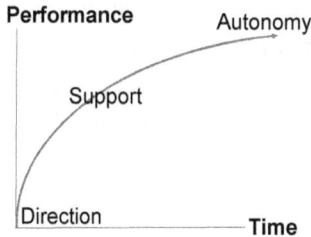

Support: In the middle of the curve, when roles and objectives are clear, support and coaching are both called for (`Harmonizer´ or `Checker´ approach).

Autonomy: High performers benefit from being left alone to get on with it along with some `Enthusiast´ recognition and reward for their high performance at the top of the curve.

Leadership summary

`Bosses´ have some obvious advantages as leaders, but good leaders have the strengths of the four types, apply them at appropriate times, and avoid their weaknesses. Our personalities lead us to react habitually, which can be dangerous when our habitual reactions no longer meet the situational requirements. To lead a meeting or be a parent for children, there are times when `Enthusiast´ energy is needed to liven things up. `Harmonizer´ support is sometimes necessary in discussions to ensure everyone is on board, and children need `Harmonizer´ facilitation when they are unwell or under pressure. `Checker´ support is required in meetings to ensure that decisions are based on facts and with children to help with schoolwork and ensure sound decisions based on sound information. There are times when `Boss´ direction is needed to keep meetings and children under control. Becoming aware of our leadership strengths and weaknesses is a big step towards improving all our skills.

6   Coaching

Personality types help us to get insights into our strengths, weaknesses and motivations, and this allows us to improve our interpersonal skills. As we improve our skills, we become more able to coach others.

How we learn skills

We assimilate factual knowledge like places in geography or dates in history with our senses by, for example, reading, looking, or listening. We learn attitudes by taking experience to heart. We learn skills, like the ability to coach, mainly by doing, as when we learn to ride a bicycle. Learning skills can also involve learning from mistakes as with falling off a bike!

Understanding processes

Life and all the things we 'do' in life are step-by-step processes, for example getting out of bed in the morning, breathing, getting dressed, eating breakfast and everything else we do until we climb back into bed at night. Most of the skills we will look at in this book are communication processes like persuasion, negotiation or giving bad news. Processes work step-by-step when the steps are in the right order and no steps are missing. As we have seen, some interpersonal 'skills', for example, leadership, are collections of abilities and skills like listening and talking. All these different skills manifest in different ways in different personality types.

I once attended a fantastic course on how to coach people to carry out new tasks. The biggest lesson I learned came with the first task, learning how to cut a sheet of window glass. I was much impressed how the coach helped me to learn to cut a sheet of glass to the required size in a few minutes, without sweat, frustration or accidental breakages.

Step by step

The coach started by demonstrating how he could cut a sheet of glass perfectly at great speed. He did it so quickly nobody could register what he did, and none of us learned how to do it. When the demonstrator cut the glass slowly, and explained what he was doing, step by step, we noted the steps, with all the steps in the right order and no steps missing. When we tried it, step by step, we became proficient glass-cutters. When we were allowed to practise and given encouragement by the coach, we remembered the steps, and we had fun. With practice, we transferred the process and the steps to our long-term memory. The ability to cut glass remained with me for years.

Since I attended that course, I've often been frustrated by people showing me at great speed how to do things on computers and smartphones. The people showing me were often brilliant, but they hadn't been on a glass cutting course and didn't show me step-by-step and slowly enough for me to follow. I didn't learn from them.

As a manager, it became clear to me that the way I learned to cut glass was a classic and simple example of how to coach step by step. The steps as shown below, call for some skills of all four personality types. When we clearly understand the process, helping people learn new skills step by step becomes a pleasure.

Coaching in five steps

1. Agree the goal (`Boss´ mode´)
2. Agree the process, step by step (`Checker´ mode)
3. Monitor learning by doing (`Harmonizer´ mode)
4. Encourage and reward (`Enthusiast´ mode)
5. Check goal is reached (`Boss´ mode)

Missing steps

We get into difficulties with interpersonal processes when steps are missing or are not in the right order. For example, in making presentations to groups, many people miss the first important step of getting the audience's attention. In selling or persuading, many people try to sell before or without finding out the needs, wants and buying motives of the person to be convinced. Another common failure in selling or persuasion is to miss the final step of asking for a commitment, usually for fear of being turned down. When giving bad news, many people fail to face up to the crucial step of delivering the bad news personally, directly and without sugaring the pill. In the process of innovation, individuals and organisations frequently become enraptured with generating ideas and fail to find the energy and resources to put the ideas into practice. With processes and especially with coaching, all the steps need to be there and in the right order and the process calls for qualities of all personality types.

7 Objectives

If you don't know where you are going, any road will get you there
—Lewis Carroll in Alice in Wonderland

Setting objectives skilfully can help us in everything we do from going shopping to building a business or buying a house. The process is described below in five steps. It may seem complicated, but we all frequently make most of these steps in routine activities in daily life like deciding what we are going to do at the weekend or what we are going to eat for supper.

The four personality types have different approaches to objective setting and their strengths are apparent on different steps as shown below.

Objective-setting in five steps
1. Vision of the desired result – `Enthusiast´ mode
2. Mission – purpose and ethics – `Harmonizer´ mode
3. Objective – logical aim – `Boss´ mode
4. Strategy – resource allocation – `Boss´ mode
5. Plan – step-by-step – `Checker´ mode

1. Vision
Visions or images motivate people to achieve success in all walks of life, including sports, art and music. Personal dreams drive successful businesses. The former head of General Electric, Jack Welch, said: "Good business leaders create a

vision, articulate the vision, passionately own the vision, and relentlessly drive it to completion." The word "vision" has to do with perception or seeing, but visions also include feelings like passion. Great visions are compelling. Martin Luther King's famous 1963 speech, "I Have a Dream!" is a powerful description of his vision for America. Athletes often envision themselves in winning situations, crossing a finishing line or standing on a podium wearing a medal.

On a mundane level, my own experience of jogging up hills tells me how a vision of myself at the top of the slope can help me find the energy to get there. We all have dreams that motivate us. Of the four types, `Enthusiasts´ are strongest on vision.

2. Mission

Missions have to do with purpose and contributing to and working for families, groups, teams, companies or society. Avis's mission slogan, 'We Try harder' is customer-oriented, as is Google's 'To organize the world's information and make it universally accessible and useful'.

Many great philosophers and religions tell us that what we do to benefit others benefits us. Some people with a mission to serve others radiate contentment and happiness.

I like the story of the visitor who commented on Mother Teresa cleaning up and caring for poor beggars: "I couldn't do that for a million dollars." Mother Teresa replied at once: "Neither could I!" Of the four types, `Harmonizers´ are strongest on missions.

3. Objectives

Peter Drucker introduced terms such as 'management by objectives' and 'knowledge worker' into the English language. He said that management by objectives works if you know the objectives and added that 90 per cent of the time, we don't know them. One reason is that we're so busy reacting to urgent short-term tasks and situations that we forget our essential long-term objectives. `Bosses´ are usually strong on objectives.

SMART objectives and the four types

Specific, Measurable, Ambitious, Realistic, Timed.

Most of us know about SMART objectives and probably understand the principles, yet we often fail to check that our goals, large and small, meet the SMART criteria. It should be evident that we need to know where we're going when we set a goal, but we often don't. The SMART criteria have a massive influence on personal motivation and are strongly related to personality type.

SMART objectives motivate us to achieve and to feel good about our achievements. With practice, it need not take a lot of time to formulate an objective and check it is SMART. We can then keep our SMART goal at the front of our mind and make sure we stick to it. If we do that, we're much more likely to achieve our goal. And, we can apply the principle to everything we do, from buying groceries to starting a new business.

Specific: Mixed objectives don't work well. You can have one goal to enjoy a holiday in France and another to learn French, or one plan to increase your salary and another to sort your time management. Keep them separate. Specific objectives motivate us to achieve SMART goals. When we reach a specific goal, we know we've made it, and we can celebrate our success.

Measurable: How will you know when you achieved your goal? "Next year I will improve my fitness" is not a measurable objective. A measurable goal is clear and specific. "Next year, I will run at least ten kilometres five times a week." With a measurable goal, you're motivated and challenged to achieve it, and you know precisely when you've reached the goal. Then you can celebrate. If you don't achieve it, then you plan to do better next time. In any case, it's about motivation. `Bosses´ and `Checkers´ set specific measurable goals.

Ambitious: Again, it's about motivation. We all like to achieve challenging, ambitious goals, especially `Enthusiasts´.

Realistic: `Bosses´ may get carried away with ambitious goals. The challenge is to demand the highest possible level of performance and still be realistic. Objectives which aren't realistic and achievable are demotivating. The challenge is to set goals that are ambitious, challenging, realistic, agreed and at the same time achievable.

Timed: SMART objectives should allow you to track progress by laying out milestones. One simple example is setting monthly milestones on the way to reaching an annual sales target. Monitoring the milestones offers a basis to manage deviations from plan.

The four types and objectives

Our four personality types have different strengths in setting and getting objectives.

'Harmonizers' often consult friends and colleagues when setting goals to make sure the goals they set are agreed upon and realistic. 'Harmonizers' like comfort and prefer goals that are reachable and avoid the risk of failure and disappointment. To 'Bosses', typical 'Harmonizers' appear unambitious when setting goals.

Bosses' are goal-oriented and determined. They set specific, measurable, ambitious goals. They are, by nature, ambitious, so they may set over-ambitious goals that may not be realistic. 'Bosses' focus on their goals and stick to them, but they can be stubborn and fail to change when goalposts move.

'Enthusiasts' like challenges and they enjoy risks, so they tend to set ambitious goals, but their goals may not always be realistic. They are creative in pursuing goals. For 'Enthusiasts', the ideas are more important than the goal or the way to the goal. They may start things and not follow up because they've moved on to another new idea and another new goal.

'Checkers' are wary of making mistakes and failing to reach objectives. They tend to be careful and set realistic goals that may well not be ambitious. They want to avoid not achieving their goals and, in general, they are more interested in the process of getting to the goal than in reaching the destination.

4. Strategy

Strategy developed historically as a branch of military leadership concerned with deploying soldiers, weapons and resources to win battles and wars. Simple examples of battle strategies are full-frontal attacks and pincer attacks from the sides or from behind. Strategy is also essential in marketing, where companies opt to win market share by deploying their resources in different ways. Some companies develop and sell superior quality products at high prices. These products are often protected by patents or advanced technology, such as pharmaceuticals, smartphones, computers, and perfumes. Others produce commodity products, such as tissue paper, convenience foods or low-end fashion in large quantities and sell them at low prices with low profit margins. A third approach is to differentiate commodity products with service and customer support to achieve a competitive advantage. In recent years many companies selected the internet as a marketing strategy instead of operating through classical retail outlets.

Strategy in everyday life

We all need a strategy in our everyday lives. For example, how do we travel to work? Do we walk or go by bike, car, bus or train? Do we decide to live near work, or in the country and spend hours each day commuting? Or work from home?

Strategic life curves or 'cycles'

Strategy is also essential in managing organisations over time. Organisations usually start with lots of energy and ideas. Start-up companies typically have `Enthusiast´ culture and `Enthusiast´ leaders. I remember feeling this strongly on visits to start-up biotechnology companies in California. You could feel the buzz of enthusiasm as you entered the door.

Typical life curves have four phases: start-up, growth, plateau, and decline. These phases are associated with the qualities of the four types as shown below.

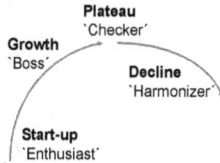

`Enthusiasts´ often start more things than they can finish, and `Enthusiast´ start-ups run the risk of going feet up if they don't quickly get some `Boss´ control orientation. However, too much control can lead to gridlock, with over-ambitious goals and cash-flow problems. Excessively `Bossy´ culture is exhausting. In the plateau or `Checker´ phase, systems and procedures are established. However, this can go too far, and excessive focus on structure and procedures leads to bureaucracy and getting lost in details. Systems and processes become more important than business results. The tail starts to wag the dog, and the organisation experiences analysis paralysis. If analysis paralysis is avoided or overcome, there is a period of success and the organisation starts to enjoy its success and be generous. This `Harmonizer´ behaviour leads to increased costs and decline.

Strategic shifts

One company I knew generated so much cash that it could afford to reward employees for turning up and getting older. Eventually, management had to make a huge strategic shift to re-establish performance and results as the basis for reward. Organisations in the decline phase often decide strategically to employ people with `Enthusiast´ and `Boss´ qualities to innovate new products, revitalize their product pipelines and get back into a growth phase. Strategic management of company life cycles is discussed in detail by Lawrence Miller in *Barbarians to Bureaucrats: Corporate Life Cycle Strategies*.

5. Planning

A detailed discussion of planning to implement strategy is way beyond the scope of this book. However, planning skills are very much related to personality types. I confirmed this point a few years ago when helping a sales team plan their territories. The team's strongest `Enthusiast´ recorded his plans hands-free on the phone while driving. He was highly successful in sales but was known to forget some commitments and his admin and paperwork were far from perfect. One female `Checker´ in the group refused to do any planning until she was at home and seated at her well-ordered desk. Two `Harmonizers´ in the team liked to do their planning together over a pub lunch. The group's champion `Boss´ focused her plans and attention on three big customers and left it up to the small customers to contact her when they needed support. The four types have different approaches to setting and getting objectives. We all have to set goals, and we can all learn from comparing our approach with the techniques of other types. At first sight, the `Boss´ may seem to have the best system, but many `Bosses´ get into severe problems because of their unwillingness to listen and change. As we have seen and will see with other skills, there are times when we all need to have the strengths of all four types.

8   Structure

Structure is a critical element in interpersonal communication. Personality types take different approaches to structure. `Bosses´ and `Checkers´ are task-oriented. They like structure. Strict `Boss´ or `Checker´ adherence to structure can be tedious. `Harmonizers´ like informality and are not so keen on structure. `Enthusiasts´ enjoy excitement and fun and find rigid structure boring and irritating.

The magic number three

Tell them what you are going to tell them, tell them and then tell them what you told them
—Folk saying

From personal experience, communications structured in threes offer three advantages for all types of communicators: Three items are easy to prepare, remember, and deliver. They also provide three benefits for the recipients: Three items are easy to understand, follow and remember. When structuring a presentation or communication, three-parts – opening, main part and conclusion – is always a safe choice. You may decide to move away from that structure, but if you have it in your head, you can return to it, and you won't get lost.

The opening can also be structured in three concise parts such as: introducing people, explaining the three-part structure, and presenting the purpose. If you aim to convince or persuade people, you can include benefits for different personality types. For example, a presentation on costs and timeframe for a new building could offer benefits for each type in the audience as follows:

1. Increase in profit for `Bosses´
2. Creation of new jobs for `Harmonizers´
3. Availability of detailed plans for `Checkers´
4. Exciting, unique new materials for `Enthusiasts´

You can split the central part of any extended communication or presentation into three simple parts such as: past, present, and future, or safety, performance, and economics; or costs, benefits, and recommendations. In your conclusion, repeat the purpose from the opening three points, confirm your goal and thank the audience for their attention.

Repetition is the mother of wisdom.
—Seneca

Conclusions on structure

Structure is essential to communication for all personality types. Task-oriented `Checkers´ and `Bosses´ like structure, but they may overdo it and become boring. `Enthusiasts´ and `Harmonizers´ are people oriented and less keen on structure. Too little structure leads to chaos. As usual all types can learn from their opposites.

`Checkers´ like detail and may need to avoid too much structure.

`Bosses´ like structure, but they are strongly goal-focused, and they need to avoid being inflexible when structure needs to be changed.

`Enthusiasts´ are exciting and fun, but they often have problems due to lack of structure

`Harmonizers´ lack the push of `Bosses´ and may be so concerned with facilitating and getting agreement that they forget the structure.

When we have a challenge with structure, structuring things in threes is easy to remember, useful and functional.

9   Giving Bad News

Giving bad news is a skill that many of us lack. The good news is we can all learn to do it professionally in a short time. I've seen many catastrophic examples of bad news given badly. I've done it myself. I wish I'd learned at an early age how to avoid unnecessary suffering by telling people things they do not want to hear, in a professional way.

With a good understanding of personality types, an understanding of the critical steps in the process of giving bad news and preferably with some practice, we can learn to deliver bad news in a few minutes. I've watched and coached hundreds of inexperienced people roleplaying giving bad news; for example, telling people they'll lose their jobs, or an important contract will be terminated. Nearly all these people made huge improvements after learning and practising a few simple rules.

Bad news can be about death, serious illness, accidents, terminating a contract or relationship, or personal problems, such as unacceptable behaviours or body odour. Giving bad news is never a pleasure. It's very often hurtful for the recipient. Most of us do it badly because we don't like to hurt people and don't know how to do it professionally. People with `Harmonizer´ tendencies care about people and want to avoid hurting them, but they're often the worst at giving bad news and cause suffering for just that reason. They do it hesitantly or don't do it at all. When bad news is given skilfully and quickly, hurt and pain are reduced, and the person receiving the bad news often feels and expresses gratitude. The person giving the news has done a difficult job well. Bad news given well can start or cement friendships.

Delivering bad news skilfully

Because many of us worry about hurting other people and feel bad when we hurt someone, we may be preoccupied with our feelings and we may think only about ourselves. To do the job well, we need to focus on the other person or persons, and talk to them and about them, not about ourselves. It's fine to say you're sorry you have bad news, but going on about your feelings is selfish and unprofessional. Looking back at my career, I'm not proud of how I gave bad news on several occasions. I'm sure I would have handled the situations better with an understanding of personality types and the rules of delivering bad news. I've heard countless examples of how people were given bad news in unprofessional and inhumane ways. The worst examples were incompetent managers firing people who had been in the same job for many years and believed they had a good relationship with their employer: "I got the news by email from someone I didn't know at Head Office"; "Someone I didn't know rang and told me I had two hours to clear my office"; "My superior of 13 years wasn't even at the meeting, and when challenged made out it was nothing to do with him." In all these cases, the responsible organisations had procedures to support people who were laid off. The sad fact remains that the responsible managers didn't have the skills or the courage to inform the affected people, directly and professionally.

Bad news as a five-step process
1. Prepare – `Checker´ mode
2. Signal – `Harmonizer´ mode
3. Deliver the news – `Boss´ mode
4. Shut up – `Harmonizer´ mode
5. Follow-up – `Boss´ mode

The critical factor in giving bad news is to get to step three quickly and deliver the information quickly and clearly

Bad News isn't wine. It doesn't improve with age.
–Colin Powell

1. Prepare to deliver the news quickly
If possible, it pays to prepare and practise what you'll say in steps two and three. Quick delivery reduces the pain, so the message must be brief and precise. Once the news is delivered, it's essential to be silent, so the recipient can absorb the information. Steps four and five are more difficult to prepare as you don't know how the other person will react to the news. As a beginner, if you practise with a critical listener or coach, on video or in front of a mirror, you're more likely to feel confident and more likely to be authentic, credible, and effective. In some cases, it may be useful to prepare follow-up and support in advance, as we will discuss in step five.

2. Signal
To deliver the news straight out without warning is unnecessarily direct and verging on brutal. Some kind of brief

warning or signal is necessary. It may also be useful to say that you don't like what you have to do. However, it's not helpful to go on about your feelings. It is the other person who is being hurt. For this step, an open, facilitating or neutral personality style is best, and if you know the person well a gesture of sympathy may be appropriate. The aim is to empathise and give them a warning in a few words, such as, "I'm very sorry, I have bad news for you" or "I have something to tell you; I'd rather not have to tell you, but you need to know". Follow the signal with a short pause, during which you make eye contact. Someone ready to listen will almost invariably look at you, especially if you look at them.

3. Deliver the news

The essence of giving bad news is to do it quickly, directly, openly and honestly. Bad news is painful, and if you do it slowly, it hurts more. A goal-getting communication style is best to get the information across without doubt or emotion. `Bosses´ know and accept it is sometimes necessary to cause pain to achieve their goals. Think of injections. Would you rather have an experienced goal-oriented nurse inject you quickly or a beginner who doesn't want to hurt you stick the needle in slowly? Whatever you do, don't try to soften the blow with wishy-washy wording. Call a spade a spade. If someone has died, say their name straight out and say they have died. If someone has a body odour problem causing difficulties in a group, say it straight and clear. If someone is going to lose their job, say they'll lose their job. You may wish it didn't need to be so, but that's not the point. Tell it straight, like it is, and get it over with directly, without emotion or any trace of doubt. Non-verbal communication is also important here. A strong and forceful goal-getting posture, leaning slightly forward, with direct eye contact and a strong, clear voice, is best. If the person picks up traces of doubt in your voice, they may start to have doubts or start questioning the bad news. It may be tempting to pass the buck and make management or someone else responsible for the bad news. All you'll achieve if you try to pass the buck is to reduce your authority and credibility. If you're in charge, you need to take responsibility.

4. Shut up

Once the bad news is out, you need to shift quickly from `Boss´ mode to being like a `Harmonizer´. Delivering the information will probably only take seconds. You've almost certainly caused hurt or pain, and you cannot be sure how the informed person will react, but it will take time to digest the news. It does not help if the bringer of bad news talks at this time, so the rule is to shut up. Watch the informed person and wait and listen like a `Harmonizer´.

People who have received bad news may be distraught and may even, in extreme cases, be liable to react with aggression or violence. They often need time to absorb and digest the bad news. It may be useful to reinforce your empathy with a sympathetic comment such as 'I'm sorry', but don't give in to the temptation to talk or try to explain until there is a clear signal. The rule is to wait until the informed person looks you in the eye and says something that initiates a discussion. Eye contact is crucial. People who have hurt feelings usually look down and avoid eye contact. When they're ready to talk, they look back up. That may only take five seconds, or it may take several minutes or longer. Speaking during this time is not productive. Silence is golden.

5. Follow-up

Depending on the news, the person and the situation, the other person's reaction may vary from mild to violent. In any case, it takes time to digest bad news. To help the person, plan and agree on appropriate follow-up action after the recipient has digested the information, but soon enough for the person to feel supported. A meeting or contact later the same day or the next morning is often appropriate. This step calls for the person giving the bad news to show goal-getting skills to arrive at and agree on actions to deal with the bad news. On this step, it may also be essential to listen carefully like a `Harmonizer´, bring ideas like an `Enthusiast´ and prepare plans like a `Checker´.

Many people find giving bad news difficult. Some find ways to avoid it. Some get nervous and make a hash of it, or they try to sugar the pill and as a result cause more hurt and damage than necessary.

Doing it right calls for the skills of at least three personality types, especially the `Boss´ ability to say something painful straight out, like a nurse giving a painful injection quickly. I know from coaching, it's relatively easy to learn the basics of giving bad news quickly, and it's very much worth the effort to learn, understand and practise the principles. We all need to deliver bad news at some time or another. Contemplating personality types has helped me and other people I have worked with to learn how to give bad news easily and quickly.

10 Giving Orders

He who pays the piper calls the tune.

–folk saying

If you're in charge or a paying customer, you call the shots and give the orders. Giving orders is a skill. If you've never had to give orders, you might think it's easy and nothing to do with personality types, but that's far from the truth.

`Bosses´ are assertive. They like to give orders. Usually, their orders are short, sharp and to the point. Strong `Bosses´ sometimes give the impression they're on the planet to push other people around. If they're in command, they decide and issue instructions quickly, which is one of their strengths. However, we've all encountered `Boss´ types who are just plain bossy and go about giving orders in a bullying way that verges on dictatorship and causes resentment.

`Enthusiasts´ are assertive and usually have no problem taking charge. Their enthusiasm is contagious. As we have seen, they are full of ideas, and they may expand orders with imaginative explanations. These expanded orders may be useful on occasions, but in some cases may be distracting or confusing. Orders are usually best kept short and simple.

`Checkers´ are not natural commanders. They usually have to learn to give orders. They're not naturally assertive, and their love of detail may lead them to issue very long instructions which lack conviction and don't work as orders.

`Harmonizers´ also often have problems giving orders. Because they seek harmony and want to avoid disagreement, they find it hard to issue concise, clear instructions. They may try so hard to get agreement to do the job that they lose authority and credibility. They need to learn that there are times when agreement is not useful, helpful or necessary. In these cases, it's much quicker and more effective to give short, sharp, clear instructions as orders.

Assertive types tend to overlook the need for consensus. Facilitating types tend to believe that consensus is always needed. `Bosses´, especially if they are inexperienced, can be too assertive, whereas inexperienced `Harmonizers´ go in the other direction, by striving too hard for participation and consultation. I once had to get this point across to several young laboratory leaders. The company had decided to cut costs on laboratory cleaning services, and scientists had to be told to clean their labs, without help, every week on a Friday afternoon. The scientists, not surprisingly, were less than joyful. Several team leaders with strong `Harmonizer´ tendencies persisted in trying to get voluntary agreement from the scientists and their assistants to do the cleaning. When we roleplayed the situation on video, it was obvious that to succeed; they had to learn to be more like `Bosses´, look the subordinates directly in the eye, be assertive, not aggressive, and tell them straight out to go to it and clean their labs.

For young inexperienced leaders, it takes courage to give orders. As with delivering bad news; preparation and practice with roleplaying in front of a mirror or on video can be a huge help. Practice helps to give us confidence, and with confidence, it becomes much more manageable. We can all learn to give orders. As we have seen, strong `Harmonizers´ and `Checkers´ need to learn to be more assertive. Some `Enthusiasts´ and `Bosses´ need to learn to be less assertive when giving orders. However, we all need first to recognise the need to learn.

11 Persuasion

Selling is not just for salespeople. We all persuade people and sell things every day. Put another way, we all want to convince customers to buy products. The customers may be our spouses, our children, our friends or our managers, and the products may be objects, projects or ideas, but we all have to sell or persuade people every day. Norman Vincent Peale described selling as two key steps; *"Find a need and fill it"*. To explain the roles of personality types we will add preparation and closing to make four steps.

Selling as a four-step process
1. Prepare: `Checker´ mode
2. Find and confirm needs and wants: `Harmonizer´ mode
3. Present a solution to fill needs: `Enthusiast´ mode
4. Close: `Boss´ mode

1. Preparation
Preparation is 80% of success. The more we know about the 'product' and the 'customer' in advance, the better our chance of success. If we know what the product offers and what the customer wants, we are in a good position to look for a way to match our product to the customer's needs and wants.

Buying motivations
People buy things partly for obvious functional reasons. For example, they buy cars to take them from one place to

another, and they buy pullovers to keep them warm. But there's more to it than that. Individuals buy a particular car, pullover, or product because it offers benefits that appeal to their buying motivations.

Buying Motivations of the four types

`Harmonizers´ are typically motivated by ease of use, safety, and comfort. Relationships are also important. To persuade a `Harmonizer´ it helps to take the time to be open and friendly and work on developing the relationship. If you can tell them that people they respect are convinced, they are more likely to be convinced. They often buy from people they see as personal friends and are strongly influenced by recommendations from people they trust. A skilful salesperson, recognizing that a customer has `Harmonizer´ characteristics, will take extra time to get to know that customer and his or her detailed needs. The skilful salesperson will also know that the needs are likely to include comfort, ease of use, safety and personal support.

`Checkers´ are interested in security, reliability and detailed information that confirms reliability and security. They want to avoid making mistakes. Warranties and guarantees can help to convince them. They like information presented slowly and carefully with attention to detail. A typical `Checker´ is likely to be tempted to buy a car model that has been shown in tests over the years to be reliable and is good value for money. Such customers are more likely to be convinced by a car salesperson who talks slowly and carefully and is fully informed on technical details, maintenance, running costs and guarantees.

'**Bosses**' want to know what's in it for them. If you can tell them a product will increase their profit and status, they'll be impressed, especially if you get straight to the point and avoid what they see as wasting time talking about unnecessary detail. 'Bosses' are likely to go for products that show their status. They like expensive brands with a quality brand image. They also want to feel they have driven a hard bargain by obtaining some kind of discount or incentive.

'**Enthusiasts**' like challenges and things that are new, different, and exciting. Typical 'Enthusiasts' have lots of ideas and will find reasons to go along with you if they think it could be exciting and see a chance to do it their way. They also like exclusivity and being the first person to do or buy something. 'Enthusiasts' like cars or pullovers that are the latest model or the latest fashion, with other features that make their choice different, interesting, exciting, and exclusive.

2. Find and confirm needs and wants
How you find the wants and needs will depend on the situation, but asking people about their interests shows interest, and most people like to be asked. We can ask about people's interests, wants and needs with open questions which begin with interrogative pronouns. What are you looking for? When will you need it? How often will you use it? Where will you keep it? Rudyard Kipling's short poem is a useful aide-memoire for interrogative pronouns to prepare open questions that help you find a customer's wants and needs.

I kept six honest serving men who taught me all I knew. Their names were What and Why and When and Where and How and Who.
—Rudyard Kipling

Benefit menu

Another way to find wants and needs is with a menu of benefits of your product or idea which suit different types.

Menu

Saves time, avoids hassle! (Harmonizer)
Saves money! (Checker)
Save more if you buy now (Boss)
Fewer problems and breakdowns (Checker)
Quality confirmed in surveys (Checker, Boss)
Reviews confirm safety (Harmonizer)
Only available to you and your group (Enthusiast)
Brand is top rated (Enthusiast, Boss)
New - the latest model (Enthusiast)
Guarantees -ongoing support (Checker)
Satisfied users - Testimonials (Harmonizer)
Status - Celebrity users ((Enthusiast, Boss)
Availability (get it here and now) (Harmonizer)
Comfort - Try it (Harmonizer)
Information - reports, tests, instructions (Checker)

You may need a specific menu for each product or idea. However, people of the same personality type seek similar benefits in all products. Customers buy what a product does for them. They are not persuaded by the product, they are persuaded by the qualities the product offers which meet their needs and wants. A branded pullover may offer the same benefits, such as high price, brand image and exclusivity as an expensive car. A comfortable sofa may offer the same benefits, in ease of use and maintenance as a new or well-maintained car.

Some of the salespeople I worked with made folders of information for their products with a benefit menu on the first cover page and sections of visual aids and detailed information about each benefit. They would show the customer the menu, ask which items appealed and then move to the section where the benefits they selected were presented in detail. If you find yourself with a product, project, or idea you want to promote, this approach is a very simple method of developing a marketing strategy and sales plan.

Confirm, check, don't assume
It is always good, when you think you know what a customer wants, to repeat what you heard, check you understood and finally ask to check you didn't miss something important. You will often find something new and important, and the act of checking can help to convince the customer you are interested. People do things for their reasons, not ours.

The more we know about a person, their personality type and their wants and needs, the better are our chances of persuading them. If we assume they want what we want, we'll almost certainly fail. As a wise guy once put it:

ASSUME, makes an ASS of U and ME.

3. Present a solution to fill needs

When you have found, checked, and confirmed the customer's wants and needs, you can use your product knowledge to select appropriate benefits to present.

How you say it

We already discussed in detail how to adapt to other types. Different personality types like information presented in different ways. That means different verbal and non-verbal communication, different words, different posture, different gestures and different volume and tone of voice. `Bosses´ and `Enthusiasts´ as we have seen, communicate assertively and like to make quick decisions, whereas `Checkers´ and `Harmonizers´ communicate slowly and need time and information or second opinions to decide. A typical `Boss´ will be convinced with two short sentences like, "With this product, your profit will increase by $10,000 next year," and, "if you decide now, I can get it to you tomorrow". To convince a `Checker´ will almost invariably take longer and demand more information and more detail. If we know the personality type in advance, we can prepare to adapt. During the communication, we can practise mirroring.

4. The close

Asking for commitment is a critical step in persuasion or selling, strongly affected by personality type. Failure to ask for the order is a common weakness of untrained or unskilled salespeople. Many people avoid asking for commitment because they fear rejection. Asking for a commitment from someone important and waiting in silence for an answer to your question takes courage. Failing to ask is a serious mistake. If you don't ask and wait, your whole effort is wasted, and you lose self-respect and the respect of the person you've been trying to persuade. Personality types make decisions in different ways. `Bosses´ and `Enthusiasts´ like to take risks and make quick decisions. `Checkers´ and `Harmonizers´ are more cautious. They avoid risks and make slow decisions. Different closes work with different types.

Alternative or choice questions
`Checkers´ and `Harmonizers´ don't like pressure. It is easier for them to choose between two positive options than to decide on one option. "Shall we deliver it or will you take it with you?" or 'Will you pay with cash or credit card" The classic choice question in relationships is "Your place or mine?"

Closed questions
Questions demanding a clear yes or no appeal to `Bosses´ and `Enthusiasts´ who like to get on with it, decide quickly and respond to short closed questions like, "Can we settle now?" or "Do we have a deal?"

Incentives
Incentives work well with all types, especially with `Bosses´ if they get the impression that they are exercising power and getting extra status and attention. "If you order now, I'll cut the price five per cent. How about that?"

Step by step

This technique can work with all types. It depends on building an agreement by offering a series of benefits that you believe the customer will go for and capping the benefits with closed questions. Several benefits are offered, and checked with simple closed questions, for example, "You stand to gain $10,000. Is that of interest?" If the answers to a series of such questions are all yeses, the person is clearly interested, and the final question asks for the order. If one response is no, it's time to start again with a new list of benefits!

'No' doesn't always mean 'no'

Many people fear being turned down when they ask for a commitment. They fail to realise that 'no' often doesn't mean 'no'. Never assume 'no' is final, and you must give up. Some customers say 'no' automatically as a habit; some do it to take time out or be provocative. So be prepared with questions to deal with a turndown. For example, by asking the customer; "What do you like about the product?" We all tend to underestimate how much most people like to be of help. Before you give up, ask one more question such as: 'What would it take to convince you?'

The joy of being persuaded by an expert

When I started work as a coach, I needed video cameras, projectors, screens, stands, microphones and so on. I made a list and set off on a tour of audio-visual suppliers. I was ready to pay as soon as I found what I wanted. I visited five stores and became more and more frustrated. All the people I asked for advice talked at great length about their products using complicated technical jargon. I left the discussions feeling confused and frustrated. These salespeople just didn't understand the basics of persuasion.

A friend organised a meeting with Manfred Mayer, Sales Manager of the largest audio-visual supplier in town. Manfred quickly solved my problem. He asked me a lot of questions, listened carefully to my answers, and showed me he had been listening, by checking he had understood. When he found out that I didn't understand technical details, he avoided talking about them. When I said I'd be carrying equipment with me on my travels by car, train and plane, he noted that the equipment needed to be robust. He also found out that the equipment should be easy to use. I told him value for money was more important to me than brand image. He picked up on my enthusiasm for new things, my urge to have the latest technology, and my readiness to take risks with new ways of working with equipment, even if I didn't understand all the jargon. Manfred instinctively identified my personality type. He made brief notes on all my wishes as I answered his questions, and then he paused, summarised what I'd told him and asked if he'd missed anything. This was a clever move as it convinced me he had listened, was interested and knew what I wanted. When I confirmed he had all my wants and needs, he told me which products, in his opinion, would best suit my needs and how they matched them. I believed him because he'd listened to me. He even offered to show me how to use the equipment. When he asked me if I wanted to buy what he recommended, my answer was a quick, "yes". I was relieved and delighted. Manfred had a new and loyal customer.

Conclusions on Persuasion

Successful selling or persuasion doesn't need to be about manipulation or pressure. At best, it's about helping people get what they need and want. A good understanding of personality types and their buying motivations is an essential base on which to build a high level of skill in selling or persuasion by finding wants and needs and filling them with matching benefits.

12 Negotiation

Negotiation is haggling over the details of a deal that is of interest to two or more parties. Negotiation often follows a sale, for example of a house, when the sale is agreed, but the terms of the deal, such as the price, handover date and other details still have to be approved. With a new job, salary and conditions may be open to negotiation. To avoid or end wars, politicians negotiate to establish and maintain peace. Parents negotiate bedtimes with their children. Personality types play an important role in negotiations.

Negotiation in three steps
1. Preparation, parameters and limits
2. Haggle and stick to the rules
3. Close (rules as for selling or persuasion)

1. Preparation, Parameters and Limits
As a first step, you need a list of the items or parameters open for negotiation, such as price, the timing of payment, penalties, guarantees, handover conditions, etc. Shrewd negotiators may identify parameters that have nothing to do with what is being negotiated. For example, they may identify the personal interests of the other negotiation party that can be of value, like art, music, or sport. An invitation to a football match might help a stubborn negotiator to bend a negotiation limit. For the key parameters, it is essential to set limits beyond which you will not go. For example, if you are buying, set a

maximum price limit and register it firmly to avoid any temptation to go beyond that level in the excitement of the negotiation. If you are selling, you need a lower limit, beyond which you will not go. These limits are sometimes called BATNAs or 'Best Alternatives to No Agreement'. These are levels beyond which you will not go under any circumstances. The other party will have limits opposite to yours. You don't know where they are, but you can do your best to find out, and you can imagine a playing field with the negotiable areas between your limits and theirs.

2. Haggle and stick to the rules

Negotiation, whether it's about a loaf of bread in a village market or a major international treaty, depends on give and take. Ideally, we want to give what is of low value to us and high value to the other side and take what is of importance to us. Some rules are summarised here as a basis for looking at the role of personality types in negotiation.

Rule 1 "If we do this, will you do that?"

Some negotiations go for years without giving or taking. Stonewalling, or refusing to move, may sometimes be appropriate. However, in everyday bargaining, to get to a result in a reasonable time, flexibility is necessary. Questions based on, "If we do this, will you do that?" can help to start the process of give and take. It's about giving what's of high value to them and low value to you and taking the opposite. `Bosses´ are goal-oriented and good at taking, but not so good at giving. `Harmonizers´ want to help and may give too quickly or too easily. The challenge is how and when to alternate styles.

Rule 2 Think big, start big, stay big

There may be rare exceptions, but in general, if you are selling and have a price range 60 to 100 and a realistic target of 70, if you start by asking for 100, you have plenty of room to haggle and end up at 70 or more. If you start with an offer of 70, you have virtually no chance to end up at 90. If the other side opens at 10, you usually need to counter at the other extreme, let's say it's 90, to have room to haggle. In the heat of negotiation and especially if you are new to negotiation, a strong opening offer may shock you, so you fall into the trap to nibble by countering with a 'salami slice' near 10, say 20 and outside your limit, instead of countering near 90.

Rule 3 Never accept the first offer

Without haggling, there is no negotiation. If you accept their first offer or the other side accepts your first offer, you will be left asking how much better you could have done if you had haggled. I once put in an offer for a house that I thought was way too low and the offer was accepted at once and was legally binding. I am sure I got a good deal, but I still wonder 30 years later if I could have got it for less.

Rule 4 Pause before countering

If you are too quick in countering, it is clear that you are not even taking time to consider what has been said and you lose credibility. Even if an offer is unrealistic, make a pause before answering to show you are listening. The assertiveness of `Bosses´ and `Enthusiasts´ needs to be balanced with the receptiveness of the other two types

Rule 5 Find wants and needs

As with selling, the more you know about the other side and their needs and wants, the better. You may find they are opera fans and talking about opera or an offer of tickets might clinch the deal, or you may know someone who can help someone on the other side with a family problem.

Rule 6 Talk interests and solutions, not positions

When we take up positions, it becomes difficult for us to change, especially for `Bosses´. Try to discuss interests and possible solutions that allow for flexibility and not positions that we tend to defend with dogmatic inflexibility. Classic examples are territorial disputes and disputes about fixed sums of money. Insisting on positions often maintains tension and hostility, which can be catastrophic, whereas moving to another parameter or a novel way forward could bring a solution. Parameters that are highly measurable like money or land can induce stubborn emotional reactions.

Rule 7 Complete the sale before negotiating the price.

I was once involved in a protracted argument over $0.5 million on a deal that cost $40 million. The real issue was whether the object had any value at all to the purchaser. The sellers got the buyers caught up in a price negotiation before all the buyers were convinced that they wanted to buy. The buyers were so pleased with their negotiation skills they paid $40 million for something that turned out to have zero value. Instead of being "roughly right" they were "precisely wrong".

Rule 8 Beware of appearances

Some smartly dressed women and men with big plush offices are rich crooks and others have no money. Some wonderful rich people appear poor and badly dressed. Veterinary practice in London taught me a big lesson. An old man with dirty clothes, dirty hands and an unshaven face regularly came to the clinic with his old dog. He had no car and asked for the dog to be treated at his home. I thought he probably couldn't afford home treatment and persuaded him to keep bringing the dog to the clinic. He arrived for the next treatment in a brand-new chauffeur-driven Rolls-Royce.

Rule 9 Never give anything for nothing.

It is fine to give a gift at the end of a negotiation to say thank you. Gifts given during negotiation may suggest weakness and reduce your credibility. Giving gifts during a negotiation can be compared to throwing food to wolves to stop them from coming after you. If you give something for free once, you give the message you'll probably do it again. It's much better to stick with haggling – "if we do this, will you do that?"

Personality and negotiation

The right mix of skills for negotiation may come in one very experienced individual, or, more likely, in a team with a combination of skills and types. A well-prepared team of two or more different types can compensate for individual weaknesses. The "poker face" of a `Boss´ is an excellent asset in negotiation, and `Bosses´ don't give in quickly. On the other hand, without some give and take, negotiations get stuck. `Bosses´ are often not good listeners and may fail to gather useful information. `Harmonizers´ are good at listening and identifying needs and wants. `Harmonizers´ may, however, give in to pressure, and they may have difficulty looking the opposition in the eye and giving a clear "no". `Harmonizers´ aren't usually the best people to open or lead negotiations, but they may be very good at taking over and playing the "nice guy" role to prevent the parties taking up and digging into positions. `Harmonizers´ are interested in people and finding out their interests and what they want. `Enthusiast´ creativity may be valuable in coming up with ideas on how to take a negotiation further, and enthusiasm to reach a deal can be very convincing. However, typical `Enthusiasts´ lack the patience to persist against poker-faced `Bosses´ or `Checkers´, who do not share their dislike of boredom and their need to reach a quick conclusion. `Checker´ skills are needed when negotiations go into detail.

The power of listening and teamwork

When I worked in management, the company I worked for, bought a sizeable chunk of a US business to strengthen the global business run from Switzerland. Our two-person negotiating team had worked together for years and had very different personalities. We can call them Tough Guy (`Boss´) and Nice Guy (`Harmonizer´). The American negotiators arrived in Switzerland the day before the negotiation was due to start. Nice Guy entertained the visitors with a tour of the city and a gourmet dinner. Nice Guy was generous and hospitable, and the group enjoyed an excellent meal. Nice Guy was a typical `Harmonizer` highly gifted in dealing with people, getting people to talk about themselves and listening carefully to what they had to say. He was genuinely interested. By the end of the evening, Nice Guy was convinced that the visitors were under instructions to sell.

The next morning, Tough Guy took charge and made clear he had to insist on reducing the price. He stuck to his statement all day, with some minor concessions on matters unrelated to the price. The final price was much lower than had initially been anticipated. The gourmet dinner had handsomely paid for itself!

Negotiating with Mr Big
One of my best coaching clients was head of a company that made and supplied chemical additives. His best customer, let's call him Mr Big, purchased a company which bought additives from my client and other suppliers. Mr Big now had two companies with the same suppliers, and he could compare the prices for additives offered by all the suppliers to the two companies. Not unsurprisingly he found some significant differences.

Big invited all suppliers to come to Paris, one after another over three days, for meetings to discuss prices. Big was a strong `Boss´ known to be a tough negotiator. My client was the biggest supplier and was invited on the last day, by which time Mr Big would have offers from other suppliers and be in a position to put pressure on my client to reduce prices. Mr Big made it clear he expected offers at least as low as the lowest prices both companies had been offered by all suppliers. My client saw that his company was likely to lose a lot of money. When he asked me for help, I suggested we meet up with his team to prepare for the meeting.

Positive thinking

I remember the despondent body language when we all met. It was an effort to be positive, but we persisted. We applied positive thinking with questions like "What's good about it?", "What could be good about it?" and "What can we learn from this?". We decided to do some video roleplays and look for ideas to make the best of the meeting in Paris. One of the team members was an amateur actor and enthusiastically took on the role of Mr Big. The exercise was a great lesson in positive thinking and positive verbal and non-verbal communication. We discussed and practised how to convince Mr Big that the lowest prices were not necessarily in his best interest. All of the participants were familiar with the personality compass. Mr Big was a typical `Boss´ and the team adopted the `Boss´ style by being assertive and non-emotional while remaining polite and helpful.

Watching the video roleplays confirmed that body language was a critical factor. At the start, team members who weren't speaking looked despondent and the actor playing Mr Big noticed this and commented on it. Instead of switching off when they weren't talking, team members practised behaving like a winning team supporting each other to reach shared goals. They listened with interest, looked at the speaker, nodded in agreement and chipped in with positive, supportive suggestions as to why collaboration and consensus on reasonable pricing were in both companies' interest. Positive comments, backed up with positive gestures from the team, showed Mr Big he was dealing with a united team. We all saw the benefits. We prepared a list of arguments to support pricing to benefit both parties and build a strong, lasting customer-supplier relationship.

The all-male team wore similar smart suits and company ties for the Paris trip and on the day, they enjoyed the discussions. At the end, Mr Big, to the team's surprise, congratulated them on their positive approach and said the meeting offered promise for future business. The driver of the car supplied by Mr Big to take the team to the airport commented on my client's team's smiles compared to the glum faces of the other groups. My client was delighted.

Successful negotiation calls for skills of several personality types. Some individuals are great negotiators, but I know from experience that I do not have the necessary patience and perseverance to negotiate alone. When there is something important to negotiate, I look for help from people with the skills I lack.

13 Derailing

Derailing is seriously losing your way in life, usually as a result of your own actions. Derailing is closely related to personality types. Understanding personality types will help you prevent yourself and people around you from derailing. If you understand personalities, you are less likely to derail and if you derail, you will be better prepared to get back on track. The following questions point to traits that can cause derailing.

`Boss´ traits - Are you stubborn or inflexible? Do you stick to goals and fail to change direction when change is needed? Can you be perceived as a bully? Do you sometimes fail to listen to people who criticise you or give you advice?

`Enthusiast´ traits - Do some people consider you to be disorganised? Do you sometimes fail to stick to objectives? Do you forget to follow through on agreed actions? Do you sometimes switch off when details are discussed? Do you start projects and sometimes fail to finish them?

`Checker´ traits - Do you tend to get over-involved in details and lose sight of the big picture? Do you worry about being criticised? Do you sometimes avoid making important decisions because you're afraid of being wrong? to avoid conflict, do you sometimes fail to say something important.

`Harmonizer´ traits - Do you have difficulty saying no? Do you sometimes agree to do things without considering the consequences? To please people or avoid conflict do you sometimes fail to speak up with important information or take on commitments you may not be able to achieve?

Two sides of a coin

Our weaknesses are the opposite sides of our strengths. Our strengths are the opposite sides of our weaknesses. Strengths turn to weaknesses and can cause serious problems when applied in inappropriate situations. This becomes very clear when we look at how the four personality types derail.

`Boss´ derailing

`Bosses´ have clear goals, make quick decisions and stick to them. These are valuable leadership strengths. `Bosses´ are committed to reaching their objectives and can be successful leaders, but they find it difficult to change direction when circumstances change and the goal changes or is moved. Strong `Bosses´ make firm, bold decisions, and stick to them, but in the end, they often overestimate their strengths and fail to listen to good advice when the goal moves.

`Bosses´ who are successful can become so used to getting their way they stop listening to their advisers. Then they fail. Single-mindedness is a strength, but when over-applied, it becomes inflexibility. `Bosses´ who learn humility and look for and listen to advice, avoid the consequences of extreme goal-getting.

I remember one `Boss´ who never learned to listen to people who told him things he didn't want to hear – for example, when he was pushing people too hard. He ended up a victim of his goal-getting. On his way to the top, he built relationships with and was advised by, two colleagues who had `Harmonizer´ skills and the ability to keep him on track. They had his trust and advised him on many occasions to stop when he was going too far. Unfortunately, promotion separated him from one `Harmonizer´ colleague, and he fell out with the other. He started to set goals that were too ambitious, fell out with his superiors and had to leave the company.

`Harmonizer´ derailing

`Harmonizers´ are friendly and diplomatic. They make friends easily. When confronted with tough, straight-talking bosses with ambitious goals, `Harmonizers´ tend to respond by trying to please. When the boss responds by increasing the demand, the `Harmonizer´ often responds by bending over backwards to please. The superior sees this as a weakness and shows his contempt by walking all over the `Harmonizer´, The `Harmonizer´, typically tries harder to please and takes on commitments she or he can't deliver, fails to meet targets and has to suffer the consequences. Instead of the harmony and recognition the `Harmonizer´ desperately wants, the reward is conflict, punishment and blame.

I had one superior with strong facilitating tendencies. He was charming and a brilliant talker and very much influenced by the opinions of the people above him. If I wanted to convince him of the value of a project, all I had to do was show him that all the top managers involved were convinced. For him, this was more important than the technical details or the bottom line. During most of his years in management, he had a close relationship with a `Boss´, who kept reminding him of the need to set challenging goals, keep a close eye on expenses and pay attention to the bottom line. When he lost contact with his adviser, his `Harmonizer´

tendencies derailed him. He allowed a team working on a very costly project to overindulge on activities and goals that were fun and nice to have, but not necessary. The project took much longer than necessary and went way over budget. He lost his job. Had he still had his `Boss´ sidekick with him, I'm sure he and the project would have survived.

`Enthusiast´ derailing

`Enthusiasts´ have lots of ideas. Start-up companies depend on them and their ideas. They love starting things, but they often start too many things and have no time to finish them. If there are not enough `Boss´ and `Checker´ skills to manage objectives, systems, procedures and financial control, start-ups often collapse, even if the ideas are excellent. Income doesn't match expenditure, and suddenly it's all over. There are many examples of new ventures started by `Enthusiasts´ collapsing in this way, but because they do not last long, they're usually quickly forgotten.

I remember an interesting example of an `Enthusiast´ derailing during my university days. Barry was good company and had a wonderful time as a student. He learned to fly as an air-force volunteer, participated in courses not related to his main subject and started lots of relationships and enjoyable side-line activities. He was active in various sports and other social activities. He regularly made plans to begin studying for exams and would tell us with gusto and enthusiasm when and how he would start. His start date was always next week, usually Tuesday. Sadly, the planned start dates never arrived. He left university without a degree after five years.

Checker´ derailing

`Checkers´ want to avoid mistakes and criticism, so they do their utmost to make sure they're right, and this means checking and rechecking details. They are strong on detail, and that's a strength, but checking takes time, so projects become delayed and go over budget. They frequently derail because their need to avoid mistakes leads them to get lost in the details and overshoot deadlines. They also find it difficult to accept risk, and eliminating risks costs time and money. They can derail when they're promoted into management jobs to reward excellent performance as technical specialists. Some `Checkers´ succeed in becoming excellent managers. Many, however, feel that, even as managers, they have to check all the details, down to the smallest expenses. They are not able to delegate and let other people check things for them. They're so busy with details, they fail to see the big picture. Excessive checking of costs and expenses or other information upsets people. A `Checker´ I knew had a successful career, successful marriage and happy, healthy children. I was shocked to hear at one point he was considering giving it all up. The marriage was an attraction of opposites. He was quiet and highly competent and she was an energetic, outgoing `Enthusiast´. They were opposite types. When they met, they fell for each other's strengths. Joy and happiness radiated from their relationship. Difficulties started when they had to manage a family as well as hold down demanding jobs. As an `Enthusiast´, she wanted to get on with her life, make fast decisions and leave the complicated issues that would slow her down and prevent her from leading a full life to her partner. His approach was to look for support and recognition of his contribution with detailed explanations. His intellect initially attracted her, but now she was busy with work and social life. She had no time for long discussions about details. And his response was to talk more about details. He became more like himself. He expected her to adapt to his style and listen and appreciate his detailed analysis and, of course, that just didn't work

Conclusions on derailing

Derailing occurs because we continue to react habitually according to our personality type when our reactions are no longer appropriate. For optimal survival, we need to learn to behave rationally and appropriately and not habitually. As we will discuss in Part Three, this means going beyond personality, finding our true inner nature and instead of reacting habitually, acting appropriately to each situation

14 Innovation

Genius is one per cent inspiration and ninety-nine per cent perspiration
—Thomas Edison

Edison, who was a prolific innovator, described genius as two steps: inspiration and perspiration, or essentially the process of identifying an idea for change and then implementing the idea. The donkeywork is in the implementation, but without the idea, there is nothing to implement.

In technically driven companies, innovating new products is crucial to survival. On one management course, the group of managers I was in, was given an exercise to develop a model of innovation. The exercise was great fun, and I kept the drawing of the model as a souvenir.

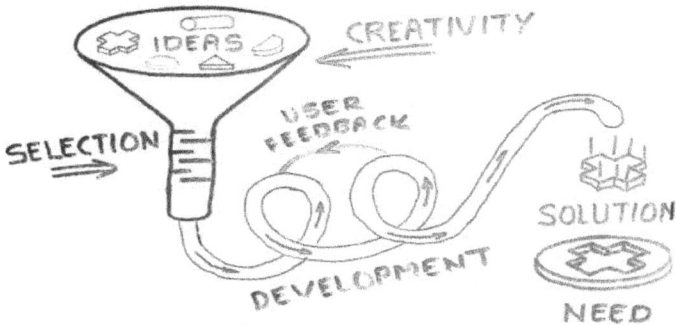

The model shows innovation as a process starting with a hole to be filled by a suitable object. Once the need is defined, ideas lead to prototypes that are produced, tested and sorted. The candidate solutions with the best results are selected, and decisions are made to invest in developing products to fulfil the need. As with most fun exercises, we learned a lot, and the drawing is a good illustration of how some companies go about the processes of research and development. From the diagram, we can identify several sub-steps of Edison's perspiration phase calling for skills of all personality types. Individuals can and do innovate and solve complex problems alone. However, teams with a range of skills and personality types are essential for complex technical innovation.

The unreasonable man or woman
In the business I worked in for 25 years, I remember a few individuals who had out-of-the-box ideas for 'blockbuster' new products, and the drive to get these ideas off the ground. They had strong `Enthusiast´ and `Boss´ tendencies. They appeared obsessed with their ideas, and they were often unwilling to conform to norms. Such people are obsessive and can be very difficult to manage. They put pressure on people to support their ideas and take shortcuts. George Bernard Shaw called these people 'unreasonable men'.

The reasonable man adapts himself to the world. The unreasonable man persists in trying to adapt the world to himself. Therefore, all progress depends upon the unreasonable man.
—George Bernard Shaw in Man and Superman

Organisations and the world need the out-of-the-box thinking that comes with unreasonable men and women. Unreasonable people are the geese that lay the golden eggs, but sadly they often end up leaving or being thrown out of the organisations they enrich. Organisations have difficulty dealing with non-conformists and learning to deal with 'unreasonable' men and women is a huge challenge for many organisations.

Innovation is not just ideas

Ideas are essential, but Edison's quote hits the nail on the head. It's the perspiration part of implementing the ideas that's hard work and often the biggest challenge. Creativity is enormously important, but it's just one per cent of it. The other part is the donkey work, where teams of different types with varied skills and strengths can be crucial. For the entire process to work, overview and leadership skills are essential

15 Attention

No attention – no communication

Many presenters fail to establish attention and contact with their audience before starting to speak. Perhaps it's due to nerves or being so busy thinking about what they are thinking. They have no awareness left to attend to their audience.

To communicate means not just talking with words, but with the qualities of the voice, with posture, gestures, and facial expression, and with the intention to get and maintain attention. Communication also means listening with ears, eyes and heart, even when you are talking. If your audience or discussion partner(s) do not look at you when you look at them, or if they are reading, writing, sorting papers, talking, or having a quiet snooze in the corner, they' re almost certainly not listening, and if they're not listening, communication does not happen. Good communicators I have met gave me the feeling that I was important and the centre of attention. The best communicators seem to me to transcend personality types. They have the presence that come from being in contact with their true nature and inner awareness.

Checkers´ and `Harmonizers´ may fail to get and keep attention because they are not assertive and communicate with less power than other types. `Bosses´ and `Enthusiasts´ fall into the trap because they are proactive and impatient, and they want to get on with delivering their message. They dislike delay and don't take time to ensure that the audience are ready to receive the message. Or they may go too fast and use too much power so that they fail to take their audience with them. To communicate, you need attention, and if you haven't got it, you need to do something to get it.

Ways of getting attention
Surprise activity such as sudden noise or banging on the table may get attention. `Enthusiasts´ are gifted attention-getters. Their energy and enthusiasm attract attention.

Asking questions get attention. When we are asked a question, especially if we think we have to answer in public, our attention level rises. The question can be rhetorical or unrelated to the topic. Our brains respond to questions by looking for an answer, and our attention level rises.

One highly effective way to get attention is with silence and inactivity. Pause, take up a `Boss´-like posture, with an intense gaze, and just wait in silence while scanning your audience for eye contact. If they're ready to listen, they will look at you. If one or two people aren't looking at you, just look at them without talking. Other people will probably look at them too, and that will get their attention. Eye contact is vital. People who are listening to you will almost always look at you. It takes courage to stand in front of a group and not say anything, but silence is golden, and it's a potent tool.

Keeping attention
`Checkers´ are good at structure, but often lack the energy and power to enthuse an audience. They may need to find ways to generate enthusiasm and energy and so keep audience

attention. I learned a valuable lesson about maintaining attention while working as a technical adviser on documentary films. The film director pepped up the storyboards by inserting surprises where audience interest might drop off. In one documentary about a disease of cows, he inserted in the middle of a section of detailed information, a brief sequence of a cow being killed in a slaughterhouse. The effect on the audience was dramatic. When you lose attention, you need to get it back, and the simplest solution is to pause and wait for eye contact to return. That takes courage, but it works.

Audience participation

Inexperienced communicators think presenting information is a one-way process. Experienced communicators involve their audience by asking questions, or by giving the audience simple tasks. The questions may be rhetorical, and the questioner may move on without getting an answer, but asking questions gets attention. If a member of the audience wants to answer at length, get back on track with a closed question such as, "Thanks for that! Can we get back to the topic now?" A simple example of a task could be asking an audience to look at the person next to them and ask them a question relevant to the topic and then ask for a show of hands on how the audience as whole reacted.

I hear, I forget; I see I understand; I do I remember
–Chinese Proverb

Dealing with interruptions

People interrupt presentations and discussions for different reasons. If you understand why they interrupt, you can deal with them more easily.

`Harmonizers´ often interrupt to clarify points they feel are not clear for them or other people. The most effective way to handle such interruptions is to explain and move on as quickly as possible.

Enthusiasts´ may interrupt for entertainment or to avoid boredom. If they are not stopped, they'll take the discussion seriously off track. If you want to keep the conversation under control, behave like an `Enthusiast´. Wind yourself up. Turn up the power, turn up the energy and prepare to show some feeling. Take back control by being assertive. If possible, make positive comments, acknowledge you heard what was said and go back to your subject with energy and enthusiasm.

`Bosses´ are control minded and will interrupt to overcome what they see as a time-wasting discussion. They may try to take control of the meeting. When that happens in your meeting, you need to go into `Boss´ mode, verbally and non-verbally, and take back control.

`Checkers´ interrupt to check details. This can be valuable, but it can turn into a detailed conversation that's irrelevant, time-wasting and boring for the other participants. To deal with this kind of interruption, try to answer briefly and, if that doesn't deal with the issue, propose a detailed discussion at another time and place.

Introduction to Part Three

Our personalities are the masks we present to the world as our appearance and habitual behaviour patterns. When we start to get behind the mask of personality and learn to act appropriately rather than habitually, we improve our interpersonal and communication skills. The part of us behind the mask is aware and knowing, and unlike the rest of us it is permanent, unmoving, and unchanging. When we see this, we see that that we are not the behaviours, habitual reactions, thoughts, and emotions that manifest as our personality. These are experiences. They are what we do or have and are permanently changing. They are not what we are. They are not the answer to the question, "Who or what am I?".

Normally constant changes in our perceptions of the outer world keep us so distracted that we find no time to look inwards and find our unchanging self. When we take time to look within, we find the unchanging awareness or consciousness that is always there and answers the question "What am I?". This is the most important question on the way to peace and happiness.

Part Three starts with summaries of self-management and positive thinking techniques that helped me to suss life. The final chapter is a summary of my progress in integrating the new way of looking at life into my everyday routine as the default setting on my mental computer.

Part Three: Happiness

16 Time Management

Small changes in the way we manage our lives can help us overcome the stress and frustration of feeling that we have too many things to do. I wish I had learned some of the following techniques much earlier in my life.

Priorities

Simple priority setting is the fastest way I know to overcome feeling overwhelmed and stressed by work. The method credited to US President Dwight Eisenhower is well known. I include it here because I find it very helpful, and I hope I can offer some useful comments. The method starts with a cross and four quadrants labelled according to urgency and importance.

Urgent and important	Urgent not important
DO	DELEGATE
Important not urgent	**Not urgent not important**
DELAY	DROP (or COMPOST)

Sorting one long list of tasks into four lists as above can make the difference, in five minutes, between feeling stressed and overworked and feeling in control. The trick lies in knowing which tasks to put in which list.

The DO IT corner is the simplest. You know you have to do these things quickly. Separating them from the others is a good start.

Putting tasks in DROP, makes space. My experience is that to reduce the number of jobs to be done, it helps to include tasks that you are not sure about, the ones that probably will be dropped but can't yet be eliminated. Make a separate pile of the papers labelled 'COMPOST'. This reduces the other piles and helps to give a feeling of control. Usually, most of the compost can be binned after a few weeks.

The DELEGATE corner gives rise to interesting opportunities and discussions. Many people think they have no power to delegate because there is nobody below them in the organisation, so they can't delegate. However, we can all delegate sideways to friends or colleagues, or upwards to management. Sending work upwards is more of an option than many people think, and some people are extremely good at it. Good delegators are usually also good at asking for help from colleagues, acquaintances and friends. Some people have or develop great skill in getting others to help them. Most people feel good when they help others, but they do it for different reasons. Different personality types will help you for their own reasons. You can do a colleague a good turn by asking for help. `Bosses´ like to show how efficient they are. `Motivators´ enjoy challenges. `Harmonizers´ just like to help and `Checkers´ like to solve tricky problems with logic.

Often the best person to ask for help is the busiest

person. Busy people are usually highly efficient and may complete a task in less time than others will take to understand what the task involves. Most of us underestimate how willing other people are to help.

The DELAY corner is where we find the tasks that really matter, essential tasks to do with long term planning, life goals, lifestyle, relationships, family, children, career, and health. These tasks are very important, but often they are not or don't appear to be urgent. Stephen Covey looks at these important non-urgent tasks in detail in his bestseller, *The 7 Habits of highly effective people*. The decision to delay is basically correct, but we all know that when we delay a task for one day, there is a huge risk we will go on delaying for far too long. Put it off until tomorrow and before you can say "Jack Flash", a year has gone. To avoid excessive DELAY, it's imperative to make timed commitments to do something about these items. They are crucial for our future. One option that worked well for me, was to plan and make sure I committed to a future appointment. The appointment could be with myself or with a partner or adviser; what mattered was the commitment.

What is really important?
One way to check what's important is to ask yourself how important it would be if you know you are going to die, say in six months, or one month or next week? If you do this, you may find your priorities change dramatically. Ideally this is also a job for an appointment with yourself to take time to ask how it would be if you die, in say a year, or six months, or next week, or tomorrow.

Posteriorities

For many years I was in charge of a group of project managers working on complex technical projects. Management reviewed the projects several times each year and set priorities. The project managers complained they had so many priority projects they had no time for routine tasks. To solve this problem, we listed posteriority projects in the order that managers should stop working on them to focus on priorities. Deciding what not to do is often more important than worrying about what you feel you have to do.

Portfolio management

A portfolio is a collection of papers. Artists have portfolios of paintings and stockbrokers have portfolios of stocks and shares for their clients. A portfolio is a useful tool to give an overview and compare related activities. When I managed project managers, my job was to supervise portfolios of similar projects. Each project and the overview of all the projects in the portfolio were summarised on one single page. These one-page overviews allowed me to compare, at a glance, the key factors of the projects in a portfolio. You can make a portfolio of any set of similar objects or activities. The overview on one page takes time, but it's worth it.

What can't be summarized on one page, has not been properly thought through, is not ready for discussion or for use as a basis for decision making.
—Attributed to Dwight Eisenhower

The Pareto Principle or 80/20 rule

My responsibility as a manager included technical support for established products and this made me aware of the 80/20 rule named after the Italian economist Vilfredo Pareto, who noted in 1896 that about 80% of the land in Italy belonged to about 20% of the population. In the business I worked in, roughly 20% of products brought in approximately 80% of sales and profit, and 80% of the products, about 20% of the profit. The same was true of the costs generated by the products sold by my company. Analysis clearly showed that some products were costing more to maintain than they contributed to profit. We applied the Pareto Principle, eliminated several products and significantly improved profitability. Once you have a group of activities in a portfolio, you can use performance indicators and tools like the Pareto Principle to make critical decisions.

Masterly inactivity

Your biggest contribution to the world today will be the five things you decide not to do.
—Notice outside a Church in California

As already noted, what we don't do can sometimes be more important than what we do. Most of us need to learn the value of inactivity. I certainly do. When things start to go wrong, for example, when the computer won't behave, I have learned to drop it and go for a short walk. Almost invariably when I get back, the problem sorts itself out. If I don't take a break, I tend to become increasingly neurotic. I have also learned that if relationships at work get very tense and discussion seems to be going round in circles, it is often helpful to take time off and get away from it. To justify the time off you may even have to invent an excuse. That may sound dishonest, but it works and I wish I'd learned to do it much sooner. Another version of masterly inactivity is attributed to Abraham Lincoln. When he was upset, he often wrote angry letters, for example, to generals who had disobeyed his orders as President of the United States. Lincoln posted the letters on the mantelpiece and left them overnight. Writing about a problem can be a therapeutic way of expressing it and lessening its impact. Some of Lincoln's letters never made it to the mail. The writing helped him fulfil his role as President.

Daily Rhythm

Some of us are larks or early birds and are at our best in the morning, and others are night creatures or owls who are most efficient and effective at the end of the day. I am definitely a lark. If I have something important to do, I'd better get on and do it at the start of the day. When I was a student, it was fashionable to work late at night. I tried to go along with the fashion, but eventually had to accept it did not work for me.

17 Positive Thinking

The Power of Positive Thinking
–Norman Vincent Peale

Attitude, skills or knowledge?

Positive thinking or attitude can improve our effectiveness and our efficiency. The mnemonic ASK – Attitude, Skills, Knowledge – raises the question of which of these three is most important for individuals, teams, and organisations. Knowledge and skills are essential, but most people agree that attitude is most important. Leadership often plays a critical role in changing attitudes, as does training. The media frequently report how changes in the leadership of businesses and sports teams improve attitude, performance and results.

As we have seen, we acquire knowledge with our senses, by seeing, or hearing. We learn skills by doing – for example, when we learn to ride a bicycle. Learning skills involves repetition and learning from mistakes, as with falling off a bike. Attitude is about taking lessons to heart and changing mindset, and it is strongly influenced by our parents, teachers, mentors, and superiors at work.

I learned my biggest lessons in positive thinking from the most negative person I ever knew. He worked in a group I managed, and regularly visited my office to complain. The range of his complaints was extensive. Company culture didn't allow me to fire him, and in retrospect, I'm grateful. I learned from him, and I like to think I may have helped him overcome some of his negativity. At first, I tried to reason and argue with him. That approach just didn't work, and our conversations always descended into negativity.

What's good about it?

Instead of reasoning, I learned to ask him questions such as "What's good about it?"; "What can we learn from it?"; "Is there some positive aspect?"; "Where's the benefit for you?". I was persistent and patient, and I slowly achieved some success in turning his thinking in a positive direction. Of course, he relapsed after a while, but we made progress.

Even more importantly, I learned to ask myself the same questions when I found myself starting to think negatively. Our minds are incredibly fickle and can often be shifted from negativity to positivity by asking for a positive answer. If you don't believe me, give it a try. Think of something that bothers you and raises negative thoughts. Now, ask yourself: "What's good about it?" There is always something.

We think we have firm opinions and sometimes we do, but our beliefs and judgments are often based on fleeting, cloud-like thoughts. A skilfully asked question can often take us away from what seemed like a firm position. Arguing with someone, on the other hand, normally stimulates new arguments and solidifies established opinions and judgments.

Turning objections to the positive

One important lesson I learned in communication training was to ignore negative objections. Salespeople I worked with often encountered objections from customers such as, "Your products are okay, but they are too expensive". Objections can be about more or less anything, from the colour of an object to its packaging, from the price to the shape or the texture, and from the quality of the beer to the shape of the bottle. We all 'sell' products, projects, or ideas, and we all encounter objections as do salespeople. Someone may say, "Yes, good idea but not now", or "I don't like the colour" or a thousand other objections. Faced with such objections, we have three options:

1. Agree, accept defeat and move on.
2. Disagree and start an argument.
3. Acknowledge and go back to the subject with a question.

With the first option, you give up and don't reach your objective. You lose the argument and credibility. With the second option, when you disagree with the other person, you make them wrong, and that's not clever. If the objection is factually wrong then, of course, you should correct it. However, these objections are nearly always about opinions, not facts, so if you disagree, the other person will almost certainly defend their comment and their ego by telling you that you're wrong. With the third option, you find out whether the objection is real or just a casual remark. If it's a serious objection, it will sooner or later come back.

When I first tried this technique, I felt uncomfortable changing the subject. I thought it was impolite not to pick up on what the other person said. However, I was amazed by how well it worked and how often the objection didn't turn out to be critical. Other objections may come later, and they may be critical, but the same rule applies: Acknowledge with a nod and a brief comment like "okay", but do not challenge the objection. Objections are made for all sorts of reasons and don't necessarily mean defeat. Some people may query or object to price because they're considering purchasing and are looking for a justification to buy. Some do it to show they're in charge and important. Some just want to take time out. With option three, if you ignore the objection, you'll find out if it is a serious problem. You can ignore a second time, but if it comes back for a third-time, experience says it's time to take it seriously.

Half-full or half-empty?

Henry Ford is reported to have said, "Whether you think you can or you think you can't, you're right." We all know optimists see the glass as half full and see problems as opportunities, while pessimists see the glass as half empty and problems as problems. I like the tale of the two sons of a no-good father. One son of the drunken ne'er-do-well became a great and good man. The other son became a drunken ne'er-do-well like his father. Both were asked the same question: "Why are you the way you are?" Both gave the same answer: "What else would you expect with a father like mine?" Both sons had the same opportunities, but for some reason, one became a worldly success, and the other became a worldly failure. Was it positive attitude that made the difference? Why did one son have it and the other not?

I have occasionally had to coach groups of people who didn't want to be coached. The members of one group had been told the day before the coaching session they would lose their jobs at the end of the month. The crossed arms and legs, grim faces and other gestures said it all. I took a few deep breaths, told myself they would all be smiling by the time they left and started asking questions to find some positives that would help them move forward. They weren't all smiling when they left, but most said they appreciated the discussion.

Parking spaces

I've read many self-help books and have enjoyed and learned from the masters of the genre such as Samuel Smiles, Dale Carnegie, Norman Vincent Peale, Wayne Dyer and Tony Robbins. For me, positive thinking is about how we can use self-help, positive attitude, and our mind's fickleness to turn other people and ourselves from negative to positive. Positive thinking has helped me keep going in my search to find the real me. One well known, simple example is looking for parking spaces (discussed in *The Secret* by Rhonda Byrne). Experience confirms that when I think I'll find a parking space and I look for one with a positive mindset, I am much more likely to find one. If we want something badly and make it part of our positive mindset, it often appears. However, my experience also tells me that motivation is fundamental and wanting things for the common good is more likely to bring happiness than wanting things for purely selfish reasons.

Mindfulness

In my business career, I had many opportunities to eat meals in expensive restaurants. Looking back, the meals I most enjoyed were simple offerings in bistros or pubs, and picnics in nature on my own or with friends. One memory stands out. I was alone on a hike in the Swiss mountains and took a break to sit on a bench and enjoy the view, with a home-made sandwich and a cup of tea from a thermos flask. I enjoyed that sandwich more than any gourmet meal. The enjoyment came from being mindful, fully present, in the present and relaxed in a beautiful, natural, and peaceful environment in line with the Zen Buddhist saying:

"Eat when you eat and sleep when you sleep." Or as I sometimes tell myself, *"The best present is to be present in the present."*

The present moment is filled with joy and happiness.
If you are attentive, you will see it
—Thich Nhat Hanh

Meditation

The word meditation has, for me, several meanings. It can describe activities such as focusing on the breath, an object, or a mantra to reduce distraction, bring the mind home and find peace and clarity. It can also describe analytical contemplation aimed at understanding the mind and its nature and functions. Most importantly, it can describe ways of resting in non-distraction, or pure awareness that are achieved by meditative activities

Yongey Mingyur Rinpoche, in *The Joy of Living*, looks at recent scientific investigation of the benefits of meditation. He cites, for example, studies by Professor Richard Davidson of the University of Wisconsin, in cooperation with Buddhist practitioners, and encouraged by the Dali Lama.

These studies have produced clear evidence that, even in very small doses of 20 minutes per day, meditation has positive effects on brain function and performance and can help us be healthier and happier. People I have coached have told me that as little as ten minutes of morning meditation helped them enjoy the day and be more effective at work. Being effective is not the main goal of meditation, but it's not a bad start.

A few deep breaths

Even if you don't have time for meditation, a few deep breaths before an important meeting, discussion or presentation can help.

Stand or sit in a relaxed posture with a straight back. Shake your limbs a couple of times to get rid of tension and put your focus on your breath, especially the outward breath. Breathe in slowly and then exhale, breathing out all your cares and worries, and repeat the process a few times.

To want or not to want?

Wanting is a fascinating subject. To want can mean desiring something we don't have, such as a new car, a holiday in the Bahamas, or something very simple like a slice of bread. Wanting can describe feelings ranging from a slight desire to an obsessive addiction, or suffering from a lack of something essential for a normal life, such as food, water or clothing.

Wanting and Dissatisfaction

When I say, "I want something", I suggest that I'm not happy or satisfied with what I have. If I'm happy, I am content with what I have and am not mentally concerned or wanting anything. Taking all the things we want to have and the things we want to avoid together in one parcel, we have the eight worldly concerns described in chapter two which give rise to our habitual behaviour patterns and our personality mask.

We all have different ideas about what makes us happy, but we all *want* to be happy. Simple logic tells us the best way to start is to try to accept things as they are, no matter how they are, and take life's difficulties along with the joys as they occur. If our wants are unrealistic and we are hoping to achieve something beyond our resources, abilities and talents, we are inviting unhappiness. We also invite unhappiness if we make people, objects, substances or activities outside of ourselves responsible for our happiness. These things are not inherently wrong. They are just not reliable sources of lasting happiness. In our materialistic, modern, western society, consumerism, advertising and social media put people, and especially young people, under ever-increasing pressure. The message is that to be normal you should want wealth, success, fame and celebrity and you should lead a glamorous life with all the trappings of fame and heavy consumption of material goods. However, we cannot all be rich and famous. And being rich and famous is no guarantee of happiness. Looked at objectively, materialism is a one-way street leading towards unhappiness, frustration, and destruction of the environment. As I see it, our world needs more people who are content with routine jobs and simple lives; people who support themselves, their rights, and other people's rights to do the same. It seems that rich and famous people who are happy, find things they are passionate about; things they like to do and do very well; their primary motivation is certainly not always to be rich. Doing what they love makes them rich.

The only way to do great work is to love what you do
—Steve Jobs

Wanting and getting are cyclical activities like itching and scratching. The more you itch, the more you scratch. The more you get what you want, the more you want. Both are cycles and the only way to end a cycle is to cut it.

Thinking makes it so
When I was 60, I went on an extended meditation retreat and was cut off from the world and all kinds of mail for a year. When I was about to leave the retreat, I learned from my accumulated mail that I had lost about half of the value of my total life savings on the stock market during the retreat. I started to worry about it. What had happened? What had I done to deserve this? I went out into nature and sat on the edge of a cliff and contemplated the vastness of the sky and the sunlight on the sea. As I reflected, a thought impressed me and made me think deeply about wanting. My loss had occurred months before I found out about it. I was completely happy as long as my retreat continued, and the news was buried in my unopened mail. It was not the loss that upset me. It was finding out and thinking about it.

For there is nothing either good or bad, but thinking makes it so
—Shakespeare in Hamlet

We all know deep down that it's our thoughts that make us happy or unhappy. My insight on the clifftop brought the point home to me. I sometimes daydream about being rich, but when I remember meditating on the cliff and being happy in my inner self, the need to be rich vanishes into space. When we fixate on wanting things, we always want more, and we can never have enough. There are plenty of examples: politicians looking for power, financiers looking for money, or drug addicts or sex addicts looking to feed their addictions and perversions. Uncontrolled wanting causes immense human suffering. The secret is to be happy with what we have.

I am content with what I have, little be it or much.
—John Bunyan *The Church Hymnary and in Pilgrim's Progress*

Success is getting what you want – happiness is wanting what you get
—Dale Carnegie

Contemplating and understanding personality types helps us to see that our worldly concerns which manifest in wanting what we don't have or wanting to be rid of what we do have, are components of our personality masks. When we see this, we can begin to look behind the mask to find our true nature, inner peace and happiness. We can stop wanting to have what we don't have and stop wanting not to have what we do have.

18 Sussing It

Know yourself
—Inscription on the Temple of Apollo at Delphi

Sussing life involves self-analysis, and that means looking into the mind. In Tibetan, the name for a Buddhist is *Nangpa* which means 'one who looks within'. I am convinced that happiness and meaning are in me and the way to happiness is in my mind. By most standards, I had a super start in life, with a happy family and an excellent education. My education helped me deal with the material world and left me time to indulge my obsession to suss life. However, it has taken me a lifetime to begin to deal with outward materialist distractions and to focus inwards and find meaning, contentment, and happiness.

The predominant world view, accepted today by the vast majority of the several billion humans on our planet, is materialistic, and holds that we are our bodies, thoughts, and emotions. According to this view, we and the world we live in are made of matter. This world view is not compatible with the results of serious, prolonged looking into our own minds.

When I contemplate personality types and look deeply into my own mind, I fail to find evidence of a separate self. I find only constantly changing experience and I see that my body is constantly changing experiences in my awareness. Everything that is not my awareness is constantly changing and although the objects of my experience appear to be solid, they do do not exist as solid matter separate from my awareness in the way I have learned to think they do.

Scientists at the forefront of sub-atomic physics also arrive at a non-materialist, non-dualistic view of awareness. Materialist thinking has brought, and continues to bring, great material benefits and it is perhaps not surprising that in this age of science and technology the world view of the great majority of human beings and of scientists has been and is fundamentally materialist. However, when I look closely and reflect on personality types and how habitual behaviours impact my way of life, it becomes obvious that the whole basis of materialism is false. Despite outward appearances, I am not made of matter, and my consciousness and personality are not emanations of my brain. I am not my thoughts, my emotions, or my habitual behaviour patterns. My thoughts, feelings and behaviours are what I do and have, not what I am. The three verbs, to be, to do and to have, embrace all human activity. Materialism is obsessed with doing and having and finds little or no time for being. To make the most of doing and having, we surely first need to be sure who we are and what we are. If we do this, it will surely help us live in harmony with each other and our environment.

For many people, their 'personality' is their true nature or inner me, a sacred possession which is part of the brain and incredibly complex. I am convinced, and I hope I have explained in the first parts of this book why I am convinced, that the mask made of behaviours that other people see as me, is not the 'real me'. As already noted, Buddha Shakyamuni taught 2500 years ago, and other great spiritual leaders have also taught, that mind has two aspects, inner awareness or knowing and outward projections such as our thoughts, emotions, sense perceptions and habitual behaviours. These are all activities or doing. They come and go and are in no way permanent. Our inner awareness is unchanging being. Our constantly changing activities are the mask we present to the world as our personality, which most of us spend our lives promoting and defending.

Being, Doing and Having

Most of the time, as I see it, most of us are so busy with this *doing* and *having* we fail to see the inner *being* aspect of our mind. We fail to see the unchanging inner element, the pure awareness which has been the same since we were born and will continue to be the same when we die. This part of us is always there. Our problem is we are so busy doing and having and thinking and feeling, we never have time *to be* and *to be aware of being*. We're blind to the mind's true, clear, unchanging, enlightened nature behind the mask of our personality.

A mask tells us more than a face
—Oscar Wilde

We all want to be happy, but many of us seek happiness in bizarre ways. Many people develop habits that seem destined to make them unhappy. They habitually want things like money, power, sex, or drugs, of which they never have enough and their wanting usually leads to chronic dissatisfaction. If they could just see that their nature is peace and happiness. It's not about learning to be. We already are. It's about seeing through the veil of doing and having, finding a chink and expanding it so that being becomes the dominant factor in our existence and our default point of view.

What Scientists say

Gifted scientists who intensively study the material universe reach high levels of self-realisation, as do spiritual masters and people who focus on mental or spiritual development. When investigating sub-atomic particles, some physicists become aware that the subject and object, the observer and what he or she observes, are made of the same stuff. This is the stuff that science calls consciousness or awareness. It is mind-stuff, not matter. These physicists arrive at a non-dualistic view of reality similar to religious contemplatives.

A human being is a part of the whole called by us universe, a part limited in time and space. He experiences himself, his thoughts and feeling as something separated from the rest, a kind of optical delusion of his consciousness. This delusion is a kind of prison for us, restricting us to our desires and to affection for a few persons nearest to us. Our task must be to free ourselves from this prison by widening our circle of compassion to embrace all – living creatures and the whole of nature in its beauty.
—Albert Einstein, In Ideas and Opinions, 1954

Modern physics is fascinating, but it is way beyond my understanding. However, I have no trouble at all to understand the message in the following quotation from Max Planck:

I regard consciousness as fundamental.
I regard matter as derivative from consciousness
—Max Planck – The Observer, 25 January 1931

This simple statement from a Nobel Laureate and founder of quantum physics expresses the point succinctly and is a basis for a whole new way of looking at life, a paradigm change.

Imagine if most of the billions of humans on Earth came to realise that human beings are all appearances in one universal consciousness. Imagine if they suddenly started to live according to the realisation that we are all consciousness or awareness. Imagine if we could see that our basic nature is to be at peace, happy and content. Perhaps, we humans could learn to live in peace with each other and in harmony with our planet. Such a paradigm change would be more significant than moving from belief in a flat earth to a round earth.

Whether I investigate the external material world as physicists do, or I investigate my mind like the contemplatives and meditators, when I persevere, I reach the conclusion that my true nature and the true nature of everything is pure awareness or consciousness. There is no separate self as most of us have been taught to believe. The fact is that we appear from and in awareness, rather than the conventional view that awareness is a manifestation of our material brains and bodies.

My path to Sussing Life

Contemplating personality types helped me get nearer to the real me and to see that the 'separate self' we regard as 'me' does not truly exist in the way we think it does. My struggle many years ago to stop cigarette-smoking also taught me lessons about 'me'. When I tried to stop smoking, I experienced addiction. I heard compelling voices saying, "just one cigarette can't do any harm". One seemed harmless, but they came in packets, and the packets cried to be emptied. Colleagues and companions told me to apply my willpower.

Free will

That raised a big question. Did I have a free will? Did I have an independent internal 'decision-maker'? Or was I a robot or machine, reacting automatically to input in the form of stimuli and information? Somehow my protestant upbringing gave me the idea that the answer was to feel guilty about my smoking habit. However, guilt only made me want to smoke more. Studying science and especially physiology with all the nervous and hormonal reflexes that control our bodily systems, made me tend to the behaviourist view that we simply react to stimuli. If my body said it was time for a cigarette, and there were no more powerful messages reaching my brain to the contrary, behaviourism told me it was time for a smoke. Thinking like a behaviourist gave me an excuse to have one more cigarette. Somehow, however, I wanted to believe in free will, but when I looked inside myself, I couldn't find any such thing. I couldn't find a separate me and I couldn't find a free will. I felt giddy, disoriented and confused. At the same time, I saw that people who act like they have free will seem to be in charge of their behaviour and be happier than people who have a behaviourist view. If we believe in willpower, we're more likely to be effective and happy.

William James, who has been described as the father of American psychology, wrote in his diary in 1870:

At any rate, I will assume for the present, until next year, that it is no illusion. My first act of free will shall be to believe in free will.
—William James

I found this quote long after I stopped smoking, but it describes well, the process by which I convinced myself to quit smoking and boost my self-respect and confidence. Philosophers have often discussed free will, and the arguments are ongoing. Many people believe in free will and never doubt it exists. For me, it's clear that life is more exciting and more enjoyable when we somehow or other believe we can take charge. I don't believe free will, in the sense of a mental entity making independent decisions, exists. I have repeatedly looked inside myself and I just can't find it. However, I still believe that the *real me* I have been searching for all my life, can take charge of my life. When I look deep in me, I do not find a self or a free will. When I focus on an object for a few minutes and then look into my mind for the looker, I am surprised. The looker is not, as I had always expected, somewhere behind my eyes, but is apparently omnipresent. That omnipresence is the *real me.*

Parts of particles
Buddhist literature that emerged in India in the first millennium of the Christian era presents a progression of Buddhist philosophy going into ever more detail, rather like

modern physics have investigated matter to find smaller and smaller particles. The development of these Buddhist views is nicely summarised in understandable modern English by Andy Karr in *Contemplating Reality*. The earliest views supported the existence of indivisible atoms or indivisible particles as the building blocks from which our world is made. Later scholars refuted this belief. One argument, that I found very convincing, is that a particle by its nature has sides and a middle. Any object that has sides and a middle can be split in two as shown by scientists who continue to build more and more sophisticated devices and discover smaller and smaller units of matter. The matter they are dividing into ever smaller particles and the instruments they use are in the mind and only appear to be made of matter. Matter is a mental concept, which can be endlessly divided. The same argument applies to time, which can be divided into ever smaller units, all of which have a start, a middle and an end. Time, too, is a mental concept.

An experiment

One experiment that I find insightful is to take a long, thin piece of paper and cut it into two, then take one half, cut it into two, and repeat the cutting until the pieces of paper are too small to cut with scissors. Then I put the paper and scissors down and move to my imagination. I continue to visualise cutting smaller and smaller halves in my imagination. At a certain stage, I get an insight that I'm not cutting paper. I'm cutting a mental concept. What I'm cutting doesn't have substantial existence. Then it dawns on me that the same was true of the 'real' paper. That paper was also in my consciousness, not 'out there' in a material world. The scissors and the paper, the chair I was sitting on, the table, the room and the rest of the entire world were not 'out there'. They were all mental appearances or concepts in my consciousness. This insight convinces me that without understanding maths or knowing anything about sub-atomic physics, I've arrived at the same conclusion as Max Planck. Matter arises from consciousness, not the other way round as so many people believe. I have also had fun doing more or less the same exercise with splitting time into ever shorter periods until I clearly see that time is just a mental concept. We have a choice between two fundamentally different viewpoints. Materialists see the world from the viewpoints of separate subjects perceiving an outside world with billions of objects. Non-materialists see the world from the temporary viewpoints of human bodies as universal infinite, eternal, non-dual consciousness

.

Selfish to selfless

Milarepa, the great Tibetan Saint, committed awful crimes in his youth. Later he found a spiritual teacher who made him follow an extremely tough spiritual path and he finally became a much-loved saint. He made the following point.

Realise the Emptiness of Things and Compassion rises in your Heart
—Milarepa

If, and when we believe we are separate entities or selves, we see other people and the world as separate objects to be liked or disliked. When we see clearly that we are all part of one divine universal consciousness, we understand the meaning of selflessness and our instinct is to feel love and compassion.

Concepts are necessary for everyday life

Mental concepts are, of course, useful and necessary in the 'material world'. Without concepts, we cannot make cars, trains, and aeroplanes and without the concept of time, we cannot run railways and airlines or make watches and clocks. The point is not to invalidate concepts, but to see them for what they are: appearances in consciousness. All concepts and all the objects in our universe are impermanent and permanently in flux. Our bodies are permanently changing at all levels. Every tiny part of our body and of the world changes constantly. A river is not the same river even for a nanosecond.

No man ever steps in the same river twice, for it's not the same river and he's not the same man
—Heraclitus

Understanding is not enough

The difficulty with my insights into particles and time is that although I at times see clearly, that I the looker and what I am looking at are part of the same united consciousness, the insight doesn't last and before I know it, I've reverted to the materialist point of view I learned as a child. To reinforce my insight, I need to keep remembering, and that's where I need help to realign my behaviour and my inner computer program with my new insights and my new world view. Intellectual insight and understanding is only the start. The understanding needs to be experienced, realised and taken to heart. For some, this may be a rapid process. For me and many others, it can take a very long time. As I once heard Tibetan Lama Ringu Tulku put it, "The longest road is from the head to the heart." The good news about it all is that if we can recognise and then stabilise our recognition of our true nature, we start to behave and live accordingly. We don't need free will. When we see the world 'as it is' and ourselves 'as we are' we start to behave accordingly and treat our world and the beings with whom we share existence. However, my experience has been that it is relatively easy to have a clear idea that I am/we are universal consciousness and not separate beings. It is a much bigger job to reach the stage where my default point of view is non-dual consciousness.

Help

Working with personality types has helped me enormously. I am convinced it can help others. My insights started with mere glimpses. I have made progress, but I still have work to do to stabilise these insights and learn to behave accordingly. For that I have needed and continue to need help.

Contemplating personality types helped me see that I am not my personality or my body mind. I have written this book in the hope that it will make this clear to me and may be of use to others. In order to complete the process of seeing who and what I truly am, I needed and still need help. I suspect we all need help. My Christian upbringing, studying Buddhism, contemplating and meditating, all have been a big help to me. My interest in Buddhism was aroused during a wonderful trekking holiday in the Himalayas. My first written introduction to Tibetan Buddhism was *The Tibetan Book of Living and Dying* by Sogyal Rinpoche. I have also learned from reading other Buddhist teachers, such as Thich Nhat Hanh, B. Alan Wallace, Matthieu Ricard, Patrul Rinpoche, Tulku Urgyen Rinpoche, Yongey Mingyur Rinpoche and others. In non-Buddhist literature, I found Eckhart Tolle's *The Power of Now* extremely helpful. My inspiration and most useful guide, in recent years, has been Rupert Spira, renowned potter and teacher of spiritual self-enquiry and non-duality. Rupert is the author of many excellent books and appears in many videos on YouTube.

It is only when we cease seeking happiness in objective experience and allow the mind to sink deeper and deeper into the heart of awareness from which it has arisen, that we begin to taste the lasting peace and fulfilment for which we have longed all our life.

—Rupert Spira in The Nature of Consciousness

Review

In **Part One,** we saw how understanding personality types improves relationships. My experience with a new boss convinced me that understanding personality types using a simple human compass with four personality types as the cardinal points could help me improve my interpersonal skills and understand myself and other people.

In **Part Two,** we looked at examples of the interpersonal skills we all need in everyday life and how the personality compass can help us recognise strengths to build on and weaknesses to overcome. Personality types are not inherently good or bad. They are based on learned behaviours that are habitual, and when circumstances change, these behaviours are often no longer appropriate. Our personalities and the habits which comprise our characters can and do change with time. We are reminded that the word personality is derived from the Latin word *persona,* meaning a mask. Our personalities are the masks we present to the world and which other people see as us.

In **Part Three**, we come to the crucial point of looking behind the mask of personality and finding our inner nature, or the 'me' with a non-dualistic world view. It has taken me half a century to make significant progress and see light at the end of the tunnel. Seeing that light encouraged me to write this book. Writing it has been of great benefit to me and I hope that others may find it interesting and useful to read.

Bibliography

Alcoholics Anonymous, *The Big Book*, Alcoholics Anonymous World Services Inc, New York, 2001

.

Buddha. *Dhammapada*, Penguin, London, 2010.

Bunyan, John. Hymn 557, *The Church Hymnary*, 1927, taken from *Pilgrim's Progress*

Burns, Robert. *Poems and Songs of Robert Burns*, Collins, London and Glasgow, 1955

Byrne, Rhonda. *The Secret*, Simon and Schuster, London 2016.

Carnegie, Dale. *How to win friends and influence people*, Pocket Books, New York, 1981.

Covey, Stephen R. *The 7 Habits of Highly Effective People*, Simon and Schuster, London, 1989.

Dalai Lama *et al*, Mind Science: An East-West Dialogue, Wisdom Publications, Somerville, Maryland, 1999.

Drucker, Peter. *The Effective Executive*, Pan Books Limited, London, 1970.

Dyer, Wayne W. *Happiness is the Way*, Hay House, London, 2019

Bibliography

Einstein, Albert. In *Ideas and Opinions*, translated by Sonja Bargmann, Crown Publishers, New York, 1954,

Jung, Carl. *Psychological Types or The Psychology of Individuation*, Kegan Paul, London, 1946.

Gladwell, Malcolm. *Blink, The Power of Thinking Without Thinking*, Penguin, London, 2006.

Karr, Andy. *Contemplating Reality*, Shambala, Boulder, Colorado, 2007

Kennedy, Gavin. *Everything is Negotiable*, Arrow Books, London, 1989.

Koestenbaum, Peter. *Leadership: The Inner Side of Greatness, A Philosophy for Leaders*, Jossey-Bass, Inc., San Francisco, California, 1991.

Miller, Lawrence. *From Barbarians to Bureaucrats: Corporate Life Cycle Strategies*, Ballantine Books, New York, 1990.

Mingyur Rinpoche. *The Joy of Living*, Harmony Books New York, 2007.

Peale, Norman Vincent. *The Power of Positive Thinking*, Fireside, New York, 2003.

Pease, Alan. *Body Language: How to Read Others' Thoughts by Their Gestures*, Sheldon Press, London, 1984.

Patrul Rinpoche. *The Words of my Perfect Teacher*, Harper Collins, New Delhi, India 1996.

Planck, Max. Article in The Observer, 25 January 1931

Ricard, Matthieu. *Plaidoyer pour les Animaux, (A Plea for the Animals)*, Allary Editions 2014.

Robbins, Anthony. *Awaken the Giant Within*, Simon and Schuster, London, 1992.

Sogyal Rinpoche. *The Tibetan Book of Living and Dying*, Random House, London, 2002.

Shaw, George Bernard. *Man and Superman*, Penguin, London, 2000.

Smiles, Samuel, *Self-Help*, Oxford University Press, Oxford, England. Reissued, 2002.

Spira, Rupert. *Presence Volumes I and II, The Art of Peace and Happiness*, Sahaja Publications, PO Box 887, Oxford OX1 9PR, England, 2016

Spira, Rupert. *The Transparency of Things*, Sahaja Publications, PO Box 887, Oxford OX1 9PR, England, 2017

Spira, Rupert. *Being Aware of Being Aware*, Sahaja Publications, PO Box 887, Oxford OX1 9PR, England, 2017.

Spira, Rupert. *The Nature of Consciousness,* Sahaja Publications, PO Box 887, Oxford OX1 9PR, England, 2017.

Thich Nhat Hanh. *Peace Is Every Step: The Path of Mindfulness in Everyday Life,* Rider, London. 2002.

Tolle, Eckhart. *The Power of Now*, Hodder and Stoughton, London, 1999

Tulku Urgyen Rinpoche. As it is, Volumes 1 and 2 Rangjung Yeshe Publications, Hong Kong. 2000.

Wallace, B. Alan. Stilling the Mind, Wisdom Publications, Somerville, Maryland, 2018.

Wallace, B. Alan. Fathoming the Mind, Wisdom Publications, Somerville, Maryland, 2018.

About the Author

Hamish Somerville was born and raised in Scotland and studied veterinary medicine at the University of Edinburgh. He worked for several years in veterinary practices in the United Kingdom with farm and companion animals and then joined the British subsidiary of a Swiss Life Sciences Company as Veterinary Adviser and UK Veterinary Technical Manager and was for ten years Head of International Veterinary Product Development in Switzerland. He has a doctorate in Veterinary Medicine from the University of Zürich.

He left Industry in his fifties to devote time to 'sussing life' which included years of meditating, contemplating and isolated retreat. At this time, he worked as an independent communication and business team coach. He developed communication skills training and teambuilding programmes based on personality types. Some key elements of these programmes are summarised in this book.

Hamish's interests apart from Sussing Life are family, history, music and contact with animals and nature.

Coaching Comments

We agreed a list of value-generating projects, got to know each other a lot better and had a great deal of fun
Harry Kirsch, Switzerland

The training helps to maintain selling skills and motivation in our sales team. We have fun, and it gives our salespeople confidence with customers
Bob Richardson, UK

A simple and effective framework that provides a fast track to assembling winning teams
Hezekiah Blake, USA

I liked how Hamish made everyone feel comfortable and open
Krisztina Keusch, Switzerland

Simple memorable methodology that is tremendously impactful in improving leadership communication
Gina Ricci, USA

We role-played a negotiation we dreaded. Preparation saved us millions, and we had fun
Ian Bryson, UK

www.ingramcontent.com/pod-product-compliance
Lightning Source LLC
Chambersburg PA
CBHW021102090426
42738CB00006B/474